INTRODUCTION: ONE WORLD BOOKS

The English language has not one but many forms. It is spoken with many different accents: for instance, Scots, Midlands, Northern, West Country, Cockney, Jamaican, Trinidadian, Nigerian, Australian. The list could be made much longer and readers can no doubt think of other accents to add to the list. People from different regions often use their own special words, with which other speakers of English may not be familiar. For instance, someone from north-east Scotland might ask a person to 'Dicht the table wi' a clout', or say that he or she was feeling 'wabbit', and a speaker from south-east England might be mystified as to the meaning. Alternatively, a northerner might not know the meaning of 'gimp' or a 'git'. There are other words such as 'billabong', 'boogoo', 'breeks', 'braw', 'akee' and 'takkies' which are known and used by English-speakers in some parts of the world and not in others. There are many, many more words and no doubt readers could extend the list themselves very easily.

What does this range and diversity of accent, vocabulary and usage mean? Does it mean that the English language is 'in decay', 'falling to bits', 'slipping'? Certainly not. The range and diversity of the English language are not new. They existed in the time of Chaucer, Shakespeare and Dr Samuel Johnson. Twentieth-century writers such as D. H. Lawrence (in a poem such as 'The Collier's Wife') and James Kirkup (in his autobiographical *The Only Child*) have shown how regional accents and vocabulary persisted in Nottingham and South Shields in their boyhoods. We should see this range and diversity as part of the richness of English, and they are particularly noticeable in spoken English. Because literature is about the way people think, feel and communicate with each other, good writing can convey very vividly the different rhythms of speech and the range of the spoken word. Many of the extracts and poems in this series of anthologies demonstrate just how diverse, and how satisfying, the range of spoken and written English can be.

A key feature of the English language, along with other world languages such as French, Spanish and Arabic, is that it is spoken and written by people of many races and many cultures. In many cases, as with the spread of French and Spanish, English was used as the language of government in far-flung parts of the British Empire. Consequently it began to be spoken and written by people in regions as far apart as the Indian sub-continent and the West African Gold Coast, and on islands as distant from each other as Ceylon and Barbados. English was also taken far beyond the shores of our island by settlers seeking their fortunes and a better life in Canada, Australia, New Zealand, South Africa and, earliest of all, North America. So English is a very widely used and a very cosmopolitan language. It is used for business, for government, for education, for news coverage, for everyday communication, and it is used by writers of poetry, prose and drama in an enormous number of countries scattered around the world. Most of these countries were once

ONE WORLD BOOKS

ONE WORLD POETS

EDITED BY

RHODRI JONES

HEINEMANN EDUCATIONAL BOOKS

Other titles in the One World series

Growing Up
Living Together: Four Television Plays
Moving On

Cover illustrations Teri Gower

Heinemann Educational Books Ltd
22 Bedford Square, London WC1B 3HH

LONDON   EDINBURGH   MELBOURNE   AUCKLAND
HONG KONG   SINGAPORE   KUALA LUMPUR
NEW DELHI   IBADAN   NAIROBI   JOHANNESBURG
PORTSMOUTH (NH)   KINGSTON

First published 1986

ISBN 0 435 10468 3

Typeset by Fakenham Photosetting Ltd, Fakenham, Norfolk
Printed and bound in Great Britain by Richard Clay Ltd. Bungay, Suffolk.

CONTENTS

British colonies and are now members of the Commonwealth of Nations.

This series of anthologies aims to bring into British classrooms the diverse voices and 'melodies' of English from the work of a wide range of English-speaking writers. Some of them live on this island, and others speak and write in English but do not call England 'home'.

There is another very important group of writers whose work is represented in these pages. These are men and women from, in the main, the Caribbean, Africa and the Indian sub-continent who have now settled in Britain. Their contribution is often distinctive and original and their view of British life is frequently from the position of an outsider or newcomer. Their work tends to reflect particular concerns: the themes of exile and the search for identity in a new, often hostile and discriminatory, society are prominent. In some instances they draw on their experiences before coming to Britain. Their language, too, often reflects the rhythms and special vocabularies of their former homes.

Certainly the range of writing now available to English-speakers and readers of English is exciting and challenging. These anthologies are intended to make the full range of writing in English accessible to British pupils. By doing so they aim to make a strong contribution to the multi-cultural curriculum. If we can only listen to these diverse voices, tuning the English language to their own distinctive use, we will surely understand ourselves and the world so much better.

INTRODUCTION: ONE WORLD POETS

Poetry written in English comes from many different parts of the world, from poets of many races and nationalities. This volume brings together ten poets from a variety of backgrounds and countries whose work deserves study and who have much of interest to say. Besides the unique view of each poet there comes also a specific view of the world dependent on the culture from which the poet comes – often a culture with many complex strands – and the history of his or her country and people.

What is presented here is only a taste of what there is, and many interesting and exciting voices have been left out. English and American poets, such as Ted Hughes, Philip Larkin, Robert Lowell, Sylvia Plath and Denise Levertov, have been excluded largely because their work is comparatively easy to obtain, and their place as poets writing in English is already assured. There are other poets with claims based on skill, originality and forcefulness who could well have been included.

The final selection was based on diversity and interest. First of all, they represent different parts of the world. Claude McKay was born in Jamaica, William Plomer in South Africa, Earle Birney in Canada, Judith Wright in Australia, Gabriel Okara in Nigeria, Dennis Brutus in Zimbabwe, James K. Baxter in New Zealand, Edward Kamau Brathwaite in Barbados, Derek

Walcott in St Lucia and Zulfikar Ghose in Pakistan.

Second, they represent a variety of different approaches to the craft of poetry, ranging from the lyricism of Claude McKay to the satire of William Plomer, from the metaphorical richness of Derek Walcott to the deceptive simplicity of Dennis Brutus.

The poets whose work is represented here speak with many voices, coming as they do from a variety of cultures and from places with often very different historical backgrounds. The differences between the backgrounds and cultures of poets such as Zulfikar Ghose and Earle Birney, or between those of Judith Wright and Gabriel Okara, might seem very great. Ghose introduces a strong sense of family life and of travel in the Indian sub-continent, Okara states what to him seem the strongest elements of African culture and balances them against aspects of Western life that he does not much care for. Judith Wright and Earle Birney might at first appear to represent voices much closer to mainstream British culture and history, yet Wright's poems express in a very intense way her feelings about the distinctively Australian landscape and people, the Australian past and its relation to what Australia is now. A poem such as 'Bullocky', her description of the old cattleman who drove his team of bullocks over long and lonely trails until at last he lost his mind and thought he was the prophet Moses, is a reminder to comfortable urban Australians that they must not forget their debt to the lonely people of the bush whose way of life has long since gone. Birney, the Canadian, writes poetry about the very un-English landscape of Canada in a poem such as 'Takakkaw Falls', and in a number of his other poems he writes of his encounters with people and places as far apart as Delhi, Port of Spain and Peru. Besides the poets' unique and different perceptions, it is true also to say that they have concerns in common – the relationships between people, the effects of history, the importance of place and landscape, the need to sympathize with those who suffer, and the need to protest.

There is much to be said for reading and studying a number of poems by the same poet. It enables the reader to gain a greater insight into the mind of the writer – his or her interests, feelings, way of using words and approach to poetry. It makes it easier to compare his or her work with that of another poet and to gain a fuller understanding of how diverse poets – and the world – can be.

Comparisons can also be made between individual poems. Many themes and subjects recur, and it would be of interest to see how different poets react to a similar situation or idea. For instance, the following poems are about animals, yet the writers often introduce different topics related to, or sparked off by, the animal or bird in the poem's title. In 'Killin' Nanny', Claude McKay links two children's very different reactions to seeing a goat killed with their actions and characters as adults; Birney in 'The Bear on the Delhi Road' describes how two men teach a bear to dance, not from sadistic pleasure but so that they can earn a small living from the bear's performance. Walcott's poem 'Oddjob, a Bull Terrier' is in some ways also a meditation on death and the fear of death. Other poems about animals and birds which register the writer's intense reactions to an encounter are Judith Wright's 'The Peacock' and 'Wounded Night-Bird'. Edward Kamau Brathwaite's 'Leopard' not only describes the strength and ferocity of the leopard, but also uses the animal as a symbol for the pain and anger in the West Indian past and the frustrations of the present. Exile, its problems and pain, are treated in different ways. Poems such as McKay's 'The Tropics in New York', 'Flame-Heart' and 'I Shall Return' are intensely, even extravagantly, nostalgic; Zulfikar Ghose's tone is much quieter, his attitude more complicated, in poems such as 'This Landscape, These People' and 'The Preservation of Landscapes'. Walcott's 'The Train' deals with exile and the question of identity if one's forefathers came from different races and cultures. Questions relating to exile and searching for a new life in an alien 'home' are explored in Brathwaite's 'The Emigrants'.

Some of the poets here use poetry as a means of stating their ideas and feelings about pressing social and political situations. Claude McKay's 'If We Must Die' was written in angry response to the race riots in North America in 1919, and 'The Lynching' and 'To the White Fiends' face the questions of racism in America. William Plomer's 'A Fall of Rock' is a quieter but very satirical statement about exploitation in the goldmines of South Africa's wealthy Witwatersrand, and 'The Victoria Falls' is again a quiet, bitingly satirical description of racial insensitivity and arrogance. Globe-trotting tourists see the Falls and think they have seen everything, but they have learnt nothing about the people who live there.

Other poems such as 'For George Lamming', 'Transistor' and 'Meeting of Strangers' (all by Earle Birney) describe meetings between people of different races, while Okara's poems such as 'Piano and Drums' and 'You Laughed and Laughed and Laughed' explore the clash of cultures that stands behind racial differences. The themes of race and oppression are voiced time and again in Dennis Brutus's sensitive political poetry, while the West Indian poet Derek Walcott looks at past oppression and slavery in the history of his region in his poem 'Ruins of a Great House'. Some of the poets in this collection look critically at the kind of education they received – education which taught them nothing positive about their own country. Brathwaite's 'Journeys' and Ghose's 'An Imperial Education' deal with this subject.

Finally, we hope that this collection demonstrates that poets are not distant, solitary, withdrawn individuals spinning out their private fancies in their private world. It is true that writers such as Brathwaite and Walcott see the artist as a solitary figure yet they, along with the other poets represented here, write about topics and ideas that affect a great number of people. Poetry is very definitely both a private *and* a public affair. We hope that the poems in this collection will give a great deal of enjoyment and will encourage discussion, even argument. Most of all we hope that the poems here will generate the writing and reciting of yet more poetry by those who read them.

ACKNOWLEDGEMENTS

Twayne Publishers, a division of G. K. Hall & Co., Boston, for 'The Tropics in New York', 'Flame-Heart', 'I Shall Return', 'Like a Strong Tree', 'The Lynching', 'If We Must Die', 'To the White Fiends' and 'The Barrier' from *Selected Poems of Claude McKay* © 1981; The Estate of William Plomer and Jonathan Cape Ltd for 'A Fall of Rock', 'The Victoria Falls', 'In the Snake Park', 'A Ticket for the Reading Room', 'Move On', 'The Dorking Thigh' and 'Headline History' from *Collected Poems* by William Plomer; Earle Birney and McClelland & Stewart for 'The Bear on the Delhi Road', 'El Greco: *Espolio*', 'For George Lamming', 'Transistor', 'Meeting of Strangers', 'Letter to a Cuzco Priest' and 'Takakkaw Falls' from *Collected Poems*, Volumes I and II, by Earle Birney; Angus & Robertson (UK) Ltd for 'Bullocky', 'Brother and Sisters', 'The Killer', 'Woman to Child', 'Old Man', 'Birds', 'The Peacock', 'Wounded Night-Bird', 'The Wagtail' and 'Remembering an Aunt' from *Collected Poems 1942–1970* by Judith Wright; Heinemann Educational Books Ltd for 'Once Upon a Time', 'Piano and Drums', 'Spirit of the Wind', 'New Year's Eve Midnight', 'You Laughed and Laughed and Laughed', 'The Mystic Drum', 'The Snowflakes Sail Gently Down' and 'Suddenly the Air Cracks' from *The Fisherman's Invocation* by Gabriel Okara; Heinemann Educational Books Ltd for ' "Cold" ', ' "The not-knowing" ', ' "It is not all terror" ', ' "Quite early one reaches a stage" ', ' "In prison" ' and ' "I remember rising one night" ' from *Letters to Martha and Other Poems from a South African Prison*, 'Somehow we survive', 'Nightsong: City', ' "It is the constant image of your face" ', 'For a Dead African' and ' "I am the tree" ' from *A Simple Lust* by Dennis Brutus; Oxford University Press for 'Elegy for an Unknown Soldier', 'Farmhand', 'The Hermit', 'Mill Girl', 'A Rope for Harry Fat', 'Mother Crawford's Boarding House', 'The Gunner's Lament' and 'The Surfman's Story' from *Collected Poems* © 1980 by James K. Baxter; Oxford University Press for 'The Emigrants' and 'South' from *Rights of Passage* © 1967, the extract from 'Ancestors', 'Ogun' and 'Leopard' from *Island* © 1969, 'Labourers' and 'Journeys' from *Other Exiles* © 1975 by Edward Kamau Brathwaite; Derek Walcott and Jonathan Cape Ltd for 'A City's Death by Fire', 'Ruins of a Great House', 'A Lesson for This Sunday', 'A Letter from Brooklyn' and 'The Train' from *In a Green Night*, 'Missing the Sea' from *Castaway*, 'Mass Man' and 'The River' from *The Gulf*, 'Oddjob, a Bull Terrier' from *Sea Grapes*; Macmillan, London and Basingstoke, for 'The Preservation of Landscapes', 'Geography Lesson' and 'Decomposition' from *Jets from Orange* by Zulfikar Ghose; Zulfikar Ghose and Anthony Sheil Associates Ltd for 'An Imperial Education' and 'In the Desert' from *The Violent West*, 'Uncle Ayub', 'The Crows', 'This Landscape, These People' and 'An Attachment to the Sun' from *The Loss of India* by Zulfikar Ghose.

We also thank the following for supplying photographs of poets:

Virago Press Ltd and Attila Kirlay for Judith Wright; Helena de la Fontaine for Zulfikar Ghose; Jonathan Cape Ltd for William Plomer; Tessa Colvin for Gabriel Okara; Oxford University Press for James K. Baxter.

CLAUDE McKAY

Claude McKay was born into a poor farming family in Jamaica in 1891 and received little formal education. *Songs of Jamaica*, his first collection of poems, mostly in Jamaican dialect, was published in 1911. McKay left Jamaica in 1912 and went to the United States to study farming but soon gave all his attention to supporting black working-class movements in the northern states. He moved to New York and from 1919 his work began to be published in several magazines of the period. He became one of the key figures associated with the flowering of black writing in the 1920s and 1930s known as the 'Harlem Renaissance'. McKay travelled widely in Europe, the Soviet Union and North Africa. In 1924 he settled in France where he wrote his major novels, *Banjo, Banana Bottom* and *Home to Harlem*, the last of which was published in 1928 and was a national bestseller in the United States that year. His early life in Jamaica is described in *My Green Hills of Jamaica* and his later travels and meetings with famous people in *A Long Way from Home*. He returned to New York in 1944 where he died a poor man, in spite of his literary successes, in 1948.

McKay is now regarded as a major early West Indian poet and novelist, one of the region's first literary exiles and one of the first to introduce sharp social and political comment into his work. McKay's dialect poems show – as does Robert Burns's use of Scots – how effective dialect can be in introducing a note of social realism, in expressing emotion and telling stories with a gusto and vividness that Standard English could hardly capture. Later poets such as Louise Bennett, Edward Kamau Brathwaite and Linton Kwesi Johnson have followed McKay's example and have further extended the range and use of dialect in their poetry.

McKay's 'English' poems are lyrical in style and often use the sonnet form. They express a love for the landscape and life of Jamaica, the nostalgic feelings of an exile, the bitterness and determination of a black man living in a white-dominated society. The best of these poems combine emotional power and craftsmanship in a manner similar to the English Romantic poets such as William Wordsworth.

QUASHIE[1] TO BUCCRA[2]

You tas'e petater[3] an' you say it sweet,
But you no know how hard we wuk fe it;
You want a basketful fe quattiewut,[4]
'Cause you no know how 'tiff[5] de bush fe cut.

De cowitch[6] under which we hab fe 'toop,[7]
De shamar[8] lyin' t'ick like pumpkin soup,
Is killin' somet'ing for a naygur[9] man;
Much less de cutlass workin' in we han'.

De sun hot like when fire ketch a town;
Shade-tree look temptin', yet we caan' lie down,
Aldough we wouldn' eben ef we could,
Causen we job must finish soon an' good.

De bush cut done, de bank dem we deh dig,
But dem caan' 'tan' sake o' we naybor pig;
For so we moul' it up he root it do'n,
An' we caan' 'peak sake o' we naybor tongue.

Aldough de vine is little, it can bear;
It wantin' not'in' but a little care:
You see petater tear up groun', you run,
You laughin', sir, you must be t'ink a fun.[10]

De fiel' pretty? It couldn't less 'an dat,[11]
We wuk de bes', an' den de lan' is fat;
We dig de row dem eben in a line,
An' keep it clean – den so it *mus'* look fine.

You tas'e petater an' you say it sweet,
But you no know how hard we wuk fe it;
Yet still de hardship always melt away
Wheneber it come roun' to reapin' day.

GLOSSARY
1 *Quashie*: a name for a person born on Sunday (from 'Kwasi' in the Ghanaian language, Twi). Sometimes used pejoratively for a country man, suggesting a foolish country bumpkin.
2 *Buccra*: white man (usually upper class).
3 *petater*: sweet potato.
4 *quattiewut*: quattie, a quarter of sixpence.
5 *'tiff*: stiff.
6 *cowitch*: a climbing vine, its beans covered with fine stinging hairs.
7 *'toop*: stoop.
8 *shamar*: a common weed that shuts its leaves together at the slightest touch. It has many other names including 'Dead and Wake', 'Shame-Lady', 'Fine Shamer'.
9 *naygur*: negro.
10 *you must be t'ink a fun*: you must think I'm exaggerating.
11 *It couldn't less 'an dat*: It couldn't be otherwise.

KILLIN' NANNY

Two little pickny[1] is watchin',
    While a goat is led to deat';
Dey are little ones of two years,
    An' know naught of badness yet.

De goat is bawlin' fe mussy,[2]
    An' de children watch de sight
As de butcher re'ch[3] his sharp knife,
    An' 'tab[4] wid all his might.

Dey see de red blood flowin';
    An' one chil' trimble an' hide
His face in de mudder's bosom,
    While t'udder look on wide-eyed.

De tears is fallin' down hotly
    From him on de mudder's knee;
De udder wid joy is starin',
    An' clappin' his han's wid glee.

When dey had forgotten Nanny,
    Grown men I see dem again;
An' de forehead of de laugher
    Was brand' wid de mark of Cain.

GLOSSARY
1 *pickny*: small children.
2 *mussy*: mercy.
3 *re'ch*: reaches for.
4 *'tab*: stabs.

THE TROPICS IN NEW YORK

Bananas ripe and green, and ginger-root,
Cocoa in pods and alligator pears,
And tangerines and mangoes and grapefruit,
Fit for the highest prize at parish fairs,

Set in the window, bringing memories
Of fruit-trees laden by low-singing rills,
And dewy dawns, and mystical blue skies
In benediction over nun-like hills.

My eyes grew dim, and I could no more gaze;
A wave of longing through my body swept,
And, hungry for the old, familiar ways,
I turned aside and bowed my head and wept.

FLAME-HEART

So much have I forgotten in ten years,
So much in ten brief years! I have forgot
What time the purple apples come to juice,
And what month brings the shy forget-me-not.
I have forgot the special, startling season
Of the pimento's flowering and fruiting;
What time of year the ground doves brown the fields
And fill the noonday with their curious fluting.
I have forgotten much, but still remember
The poinsettia's red, blood-red in warm December.

I still recall the honey-fever grass,
But cannot recollect the high days when
We rooted them out of the ping-wing path
To stop the mad bees in the rabbit pen.
I often try to think in what sweet month
The languid painted ladies used to dapple
The yellow by-road mazing from the main,
Sweet with the golden threads of the rose-apple.
I have forgotten – strange – but quite remember
The poinsettia's red, blood-red in warm December.

What weeks, what months, what time of the mild year
We cheated school to have our fling at tops?
What days our wine-thrilled bodies pulsed with joy
Feasting upon blackberries in the copse?
Oh some I know! I have embalmed the days,
Even the sacred moments when we played,
All innocent of passion, uncorrupt,
At noon and evening in the flame-heart's shade.
We were so happy, happy, I remember,
Beneath the poinsettia's red in warm December.

I SHALL RETURN

I shall return again. I shall return
To laugh and love and watch with wonder-eyes
At golden noon the forest fires burn,
Wafting their blue-black smoke to sapphire skies.
I shall return to loiter by the streams
That bathe the brown blades of the bending grasses,
And realize once more my thousand dreams
Of waters rushing down the mountain passes.
I shall return to hear the fiddle and fife
Of village dances, dear delicious tunes
That stir the hidden depths of native life,
Stray melodies of dim-remembered tunes.
I shall return. I shall return again
To ease my mind of long, long years of pain.

LIKE A STRONG TREE

Like a strong tree that in the virgin earth
Sends far its roots through rock and loam and clay,
And proudly thrives in rain or time of dearth,
When dry waves scare the rain-come sprites away;
Like a strong tree that reaches down deep, deep,
For sunken water, fluid underground,
Where the great-ringed unsightly blind worms creep,
And queer things of the nether world abound:

So would I live in rich imperial growth,
Touching the surface and the depth of things,
Instinctively responsive unto both,
Tasting the sweets of being, fearing no stings,
Sensing the subtle spell of changing forms,
Like a strong tree against a thousand storms.

THE LYNCHING

His spirit in smoke ascended to high heaven.
His father, by the cruellest way of pain,
Had bidden him to his bosom once again;
The awful sin remained still unforgiven.
All night a bright and solitary star
(Perchance the one that ever guided him,
Yet gave him up at last to Fate's wild whim)
Hung pitifully o'er the swinging char.
Day dawned, and soon the mixed crowds came to view
The ghastly body swaying in the sun:
The women thronged to look, but never a one
Showed sorrow in her eyes of steely blue;
And little lads, lynchers that were to be,
Danced round the dreadful thing in fiendish glee.

IF WE MUST DIE

If we must die – let it not be like hogs
Hunted and penned in an inglorious spot,
While round us bark the mad and hungry dogs,
Making their mock at our accursed lot.
If we must die – oh, let us nobly die,
So that our precious blood may not be shed
In vain; then even the monsters we defy
Shall be constrained to honour us though dead!
Oh, Kinsmen! We must meet the common foe;
Though far outnumbered, let us show us brave,
And for their thousand blows deal one death-blow!
What though before us lies the open grave?

Like men we'll face the murderous, cowardly pack,
Pressed to the wall, dying, but fighting back!

FOOTNOTE
This sonnet was inspired by the race riots that occurred in various cities in the USA in
1919.

TO THE WHITE FIENDS

Think you I am not fiend and savage too?
Think you I could not arm me with a gun
And shoot down ten of you for every one
Of my black brothers murdered, burnt by you?
Be not deceived, for every deed you do
I could match – out-match: am I not Africa's son,
Black of that black land where black deeds are done?
But the Almighty from the darkness drew
My soul and said: Even thou shalt be a light
Awhile to burn on the benighted earth,
Thy dusky face I set among the white
For thee to prove thyself of highest worth;
Before the world is swallowed up in night,
To show thy little lamp: go forth, go forth!

THE BARRIER

I must not gaze at them although
Your eyes are dawning day;
I must not watch you as you go
Your sun-illumined way.

I hear but I must never heed
The fascinating note,
Which, fluting like a river reed,
Comes from your trembling throat.

I must not see upon your face
Love's softly glowing spark;
For there's the barrier of race,
You're fair and I am dark.

SUGGESTIONS FOR WRITING AND DISCUSSION

1 *Using the poems selected here, illustrate the kinds of subject McKay wrote about.*
2 *Choose two of McKay's sonnets and show how he used the sonnet form.*
3 *McKay is 'a poet of protest and rebellion'. Judging from the poems selected here, how true would you say this statement is?*
4 *Justify the description of McKay as 'a lyric poet'.*
5 *Read aloud the two dialect poems 'Quashie to Buccra' and 'Killin' Nanny'. What do you think is gained by writing in dialect? What, if anything, is lost?*
6 *Do you think poetry is a good medium for registering protest? Can you think of any present-day singers or poets who use songs and poems as a medium for protest? What issues/topics of today do you think could be written or sung about? (Pollution, black–white relations, bad housing, unemployment, famine?) On your own or in groups try composing a protest poem or song for taping or class performance.*
7 'The Tropics in New York', 'Flame-Heart', 'I Shall Return'. *Each of these poems expresses a sense of nostalgia, exile, longing. Think of a place where you once lived, or visited, where you were very happy (it could be in the town or country). List the sights, sounds, smells and people you remember. Then write your own poem – you could call it 'Memory', or perhaps by the name of the place you are remembering. Before you start, look carefully at the way McKay uses rhyme, and how he selects details of what he is describing.*

FURTHER READING

Selected Poems Claude McKay (Twayne Publishers)
My Green Hills of Jamaica Claude McKay (Heinemann Educational Books)
A Long Way from Home Claude McKay (Pluto Press)
Banjo Claude McKay (Harcourt Brace Jovanovich, New York)
Banana Bottom Claude McKay (Harcourt Brace Jovanovich, New York)
Jamaica Labrish Louise Bennett (Collins & Sangster, Jamaica)
Dread Beat and Blood Linton Kwesi Johnson (Bogle L'Ouverture)

WILLIAM PLOMER

William Plomer was born in a small town in the Transvaal, South Africa, in 1903. He was educated in England and returned to South Africa where he was, for a while, a farmer. He then lived for a short time in Johannesburg and after that became a trader in Zululand. He wrote his first novel, *Turbott Wolfe*, at the age of eighteen and sent the pencil-written manuscript to the Hogarth Press in London where it was accepted for publication. He became joint editor (with Roy Campbell and Laurens van der Post) of the avant-garde and anti-establishment literary magazine *Voorslag* in 1928. However, he soon left South Africa and spent some years in Japan. He then travelled in Europe, lived for a time in Spain, and finally settled in England where he was a

reviewer, broadcaster and editor. As well as poetry and novels, Plomer wrote short stories, biographies and the librettos for a number of operas by Benjamin Britten, including *Gloriana*. He won many awards for his poetry and was President of the Poetry Society from 1968 to 1971. He died in 1973.

Plomer's early South African poems are often very critical of conventional white attitudes to black people. He has a feeling for places, for the absurdity of people's behaviour, and for the strange and the macabre. Much of his poetry is satirical, his effects being gained by the witty use of the telling image, the neat rhyme and irony. But he feels compassion, too, for those who cannot or do not conform to society's demands (as in 'Move On').

A FALL OF ROCK

Where not so long ago the breezes stirred
The summer grasses, now
A fat contralto gargles for applause
And bows in sequins when the curtain falls.

A sudden tremor shakes the theatre
And 'Oh!' cry two or three, while red and blue
Sparks fly from diamond earrings; several men
Are glad of an excuse to squeeze white hands
And murmur reassurance in small ears.
They say perhaps it was a fall of rock
In the deep mines below.

Perhaps it was a fall of rock. The city stands[1]
On shafts and tunnels and a stinking void,
The bright enamel of a hollow tooth.
Where springbok bounded screams the tram,
And lawyer, politician, magnate sit
Where kite and vulture flew and fed.
Where the snake sunned itself, white children play;
Where wildebeest drank, a church is built.

Perhaps it was a fall of rock. Two kaffirs[2] trapped
Up to the waist in dirty water. All the care
That went to keep them fit—!
Concrete bathrooms and carbolic soap,

A balanced diet and free hospitals
Made them efficient, but they die alone.
Half stunned, then drowned,
They might have lived in the sun
With miner's phthisis, silicosis,
A gradual petrifaction of the lungs.

If anybody imagines that ever
All this will come to an end,
That the jackal will howl on the ruined terraces
Of this city where science is applied for profit
And where the roar of machinery by night and day
Is louder than the beating of all the hearts of the inhabitants,
Far louder than the quiet voice of common sense;
If anybody should think that a mile below ground
The moling and maggoting will cease, or console himself
For his own failure to share the life of the city
With romantic hopes for its ruin,
He is wasting his time.

Do not let him suppose
That a bad future avenges the wrongs of now,
And let him remember
There is a fine gold to be won
By not always knowing best.

GLOSSARY
1 *The city stands*: Johannesburg is built, in many parts, over gold mines. Gold was discovered there in 1867.
2 *kaffirs*: 'kaffir' is a word used for South African blacks by Afrikaans-speakers. It is now regarded as an offensive and highly insulting term.

THE VICTORIA FALLS

These are the Victoria Falls,[1] whose noisy gushing
Attracts a noisy and a gushing crowd
Who rush from every country in the world to gape
At this cascade that is the usual shape.

Over the brink a lot of water slops
By force of gravity, and many a tourist stops
And stares to see a natural law fulfilled
And quantities of water that never stop being spilled.

These are the Victoria Falls, the brightest trinket
In the globe-trotter's box of well-worn curios:
If they want water, good God, let them drink it!
If they want falls, we'll knock them down – here goes!

Why do you come, I wonder, all this weary way?
Is it because you like to smile and say
'When we were at the Falls the other day—'?
Is it because you like to see the spray?

Is it because you like to feel how far
It is from Boston to these falls of the Zambesi,
Which must be falling still? Or do you feel uneasy
Until you know how like their photograph they are?

A female tourist raves, 'We're keen as keen
On Africa! It's dusty – but, my dear, the *sun*!
I had a list of all the things we've seen,
I can't remember half the things we've done!

'The Kaffirs? Black as black, they live in such quaint kraals[2] –
They're dusty, too! The great thing is to see the Falls,
The rainbows, and the Rain Forest, where we all wore mackintoshes,
Admired the ferns, and were so glad we'd all brought our goloshes!'

(The water spirits leered at her, the lurking *tokoloshes*.[3])
'My dear, the spray! the noise! the view! the beautiful hotel!
Electric light in every room, and an electric bell!
So clean and comfortable, and they looked after us so well!'

She will not go away . . . Ach, I long to be alone
With a guide-book to the gentle Falls of Silence,
The Temple of Reticence on the Tranquil Islands,
Where no sound enters, whence no sound goes out,
And waterfalls
    Fall
      Quietly,
        As tea falls
          From
            A spout.

GLOSSARY

1 *Victoria Falls*: the Falls are on the border of present-day Zimbabwe and Zambia.
2 *kraals*: 'kraal' is the Afrikaans word given to a South African village of huts enclosed
  by a fence.
3 *tokoloshes*: 'mischievous or malignant bogies or goblins in Bantu mythology' (poet's
  note).

IN THE SNAKE PARK

A white-hot midday in the Snake Park.
Lethargy lay here and there in coils,
And here and there a neat obsidian[1] head
Lay dreaming on a plaited pillow of its own
Loops like a pretzel or a true-love-knot.

A giant Python seemed a heap of tyres;
Two Nielsen's Vipers looked for a way out,
Sick of their cage and one another's curves;
And the long Ringsnake brought from Lembuland
Poured slowly through an opening like smoke.

Leaning intently forward a young girl
Discerned in stagnant water on a rock
A dark brown shoestring or discarded whiplash,
Then read the label to find out the name,
Then stared again: it moved. She screamed.

Old Piet Vander leant with us that day
On the low wall around the rocky space
Where amid broken quartz that cast no shade
Snakes twitched or slithered, or appeared to sleep,
Or lay invisible in the singing glare.

The sun throbbed like a fever as he spoke:
'Look carefully at this shrub with glossy leaves.'
Leaves bright as brass. 'That leaf on top
Just there, do you see that it has eyes?
That's a Green Mamba, and it's watching *you*.

'A man I once knew did survive the bite,
Saved by a doctor running with a knife,
Serum and all. He was never the same again.
Vomiting blackness, agonizing, passing blood,
Part paralysed, near gone, he felt

'(He told me later) he would burst apart;
But the worst agony was in his mind –
Unbearable nightmare, worse than total grief
Or final loss of hope, impossibly magnified
To a blind passion of panic and extreme distress.'

'Why should that little head have power
To inject all horror for no reason at all?'
'Ask me another – and beware of snakes.'
The sun was like a burning-glass. Face down
The girl who screamed had fallen in a faint.

GLOSSARY
1 *obsidian*: dark vitreous lava or volcanic rock-like bottle-glass.

A TICKET FOR THE READING ROOM

With a smile of secret triumph
  Seedy old untidy scholar,
Inkstains on his fingernails,
  Cobwebs on his Gladstone collar,

Down at heel and out at elbows
  Off he goes on gouty feet
(Where he goes his foxy smell goes),
  Off towards Great Russell Street.[1]

Unaware of other people,
  Peace and war and politics,
Down the pavement see him totter
  Following his *idée fixe*.[2]

Past the rowdy corner café
  Full of Cypriots and flies
Where the customers see daggers
  Looking from each other's eyes,

Past the sad but so-called Fun Fair
  Where a few immortal souls
Occupy their leisure hours
  Shooting little balls at holes,

Past the window full of booklets,
  Rubber goods and cures for piles,
Past the pub, the natty milk-bar
  Crowded with galactophiles,

Through the traffic, down the side-street
  Where an unfrocked parson thrives
('Palmist and Psychologist')
  Cutting short unwanted lives,

Through the shady residential
    Square in which a widow runs
A quiet gambling-hell, or 'bridge club',
    Fleecing other women's sons,

On he shuffles, quietly mumbling
    Figures, facts and formulae –
Bats are busy in the belfry,
    In the bonnet hums a bee.

At the Reading Room he settles
    Pince-nez on his bottle nose,
Reads and scribbles, reads and scribbles,
    Till the day draws to a close,

Then returns to oh, what squalor!
    Kippers, cake and dark brown tea,
Filthy sheets and filthier blankets,
    Sleep disturbed by mouse and flea.

What has the old man been doing?
    What's his game? Another book?
He is out to pour contempt on
    Esperanto, Volapük,

To fake a universal language
    Full of deft abbreviation
For the day when all mankind
    Join and form one happy nation.

In this the poor chap resembles
    Prosperous idealists
Who talk as if men reached for concord
    With their clenched or grasping fists.

GLOSSARY
1 *Great Russell Street*: the British Museum, to which the Reading Room belongs, is
in Great Russell Street, London.
2 *idée fixe*: obsession.

MOVE ON

They made love under bridges, lacking beds,
And engines whistled them a bridal song,
A sudden bull's-eye showed them touching heads,
Policemen told them they were doing wrong;

And when they slept on seats in public gardens
Told them, 'Commit no nuisance in the park';
The beggars, begging the policemen's pardons,
Said that they thought as it was after dark –

At this the law grew angry and declared
Outlaws who outrage by-laws are the devil;
At this the lovers only stood and stared,
As well they might, for they had meant no evil;
'Move on,' the law said. To avoid a scene
They moved. And thus we keep our cities clean.

THE DORKING[1] THIGH

About to marry and invest
Their lives in safety and routine
Stanley and June required a nest
And came down on the 4.15.

The agent drove them to the Posh Estate
And showed them several habitations.
None did. The afternoon got late
With questions, doubts, and explanations.

Then day grew dim and Stan fatigued
And disappointment raised its head,
But June declared herself intrigued
To know where that last turning led.

It led to a Tudor snuggery styled
'Ye Kumfi Nooklet' on the gate.
'A gem of a home,' the salesman smiled,
'My pet place on the whole estate;

'It's not quite finished, but you'll see
Good taste itself.' They went inside.
'This little place is built to be
A husband's joy, a housewife's pride.'

They saw the white convenient sink,
The modernistic chimneypiece,
June gasped for joy, Stan gave a wink
To say, 'Well, here our quest can cease.'

The salesman purred (he'd managed well)
And June undid a cupboard door.
'For linen,' she beamed. And out there fell
A nameless Something on the floor.

'Something the workmen left, I expect,'
The agent said, as it fell at his feet,
Nor knew that his chance of a sale was wrecked.
'Good heavens, it must be a joint of meat!'

Ah yes, it was meat, it was meat all right,
A joint those three will never forget –
For they stood alone in the Surrey night
With the severed thigh of a plump brunette . . .

                *   *   *

Early and late, early and late,
Traffic was jammed round the Posh Estate,
And the papers were full of the Dorking Thigh
And who, and when, and where, and why.

A trouser button was found in the mud.
(Who made it? Who wore it? Who lost it? Who knows?)
But no one found a trace of blood
Or her body or face, or the spoiler of those.

He's acting a play in the common air
On which no curtain can ever come down.
Though 'Ye Kumfi Nooklet' was shifted elsewhere
June made Stan take a flat in town.

GLOSSARY
1 *Dorking*: a town in Surrey favoured by commuters working in London and regarded as being respectable and middle class.

HEADLINE HISTORY

GRAVE CHARGE IN MAYFAIR BATHROOM CASE,
ROMAN REMAINS FOR MIDDLE WEST,
GOLFING BISHOP CALLS FOR PRAYERS,
HOW MURDERED BRIDE WAS DRESSED,

BOXER INSURES HIS JOIE-DE-VIVRE,
DUCHESS DENIES THAT VAMPS ARE VAIN,
DO WOMEN MAKE GOOD WIVES?
GIANT AIRSHIP OVER SPAIN,

SOPRANO SINGS FOR FORTY HOURS,
COCKTAIL BAR ON MOORING MAST,
'NOISE, MORE NOISE!' POET'S LAST WORDS,
COMPULSORY WIRELESS BILL IS PASSED,

ALLEGED LAST TRUMP BLOWN YESTERDAY,
TRAFFIC DROWNS CALL TO QUICK AND DEAD,
CUP TIE CROWD SEES HEAVENS OPE,
'NOT END OF WORLD', SAYS WELL-KNOWN RED.

POET'S NOTE
'One or two period details here may now be obscure. Vamps were coquettes, and the mooring mast was for the benefit of giant airships, for some years thought to have a future.'

SUGGESTIONS FOR WRITING AND DISCUSSION

1 *Using the poems selected here, illustrate the kinds of subject that Plomer satirized, for example, exploitation of men and labour, shallow tourists, useless scholars, selfishness.*
2 *Illustrate Plomer's skill as a satirist by close examination of two of his poems.*
3 *'Plomer ridicules the foibles of his fellow man, but he also feels compassion.' How true do you think this statement is?*
4 *Choose one of the characters Plomer writes about. Re-tell his or her story in his or her own words.*
5 *'A Fall of Rock'. Imagine that the 'Two kaffirs trapped/Up to the waist in dirty water' have the chance to speak and put their case to the white Johannesburg theatre audience. Write (and then perhaps act) your version of the dialogue that takes place.*
6 *'Headline History'. List the different kinds of 'history' that the headlines record. Try a similar 'Headline History' poem for today. (You could choose and perhaps re-word headlines from local and national newspapers and arrange them in the order you think best.)*
7 *Write your own verses to follow on from the end of 'In the Snake Park' or 'The Dorking Thigh'. (You could say what happens to the girl 'who had fallen in a faint' and what the murderer does next in 'The Dorking Thigh'.)*

FURTHER READING

Collected Poems William Plomer (Jonathan Cape)

EARLE BIRNEY

Earle Birney was born in
Calgary, Canada, in 1904. He
was brought up in the
mountainous regions of Alberta
and British Columbia. He was
educated at the University of
British Columbia and later
became Professor of English
there. During the Second World
War he served in the Canadian
Army, attaining the rank of
major, and fought in Belgium
and Holland. He has edited
numerous creative and literary
magazines. He was a close
friend of the poet and writer
Malcolm Lowry, author of
Under the Volcano.

Birney's poetry shows a delight
in playing with language,
typography and punctuation
which can be compared in some
ways with that of the American
poet e. e. cummings. Birney
ironically quotes one of his

critics as saying of his poems: 'The typewriter roller was wobbly, and the shift-key wasn't working properly.' The subjects for his poems are clearly inspired by his travels, incidents that happened to him, and people he met, as well as by his social conscience.

THE BEAR ON THE DELHI ROAD

Unreal   tall as a myth
by the road the Himalayan bear
is beating the brilliant air
with his crooked arms
About him two men   bare
spindly as locusts   leap

One pulls on a ring
in the great soft nose   His mate
flicks   flicks with a stick
up at the rolling eyes

They have not led him here
down from the fabulous hills
to this bald alien plain
and the clamorous world   to kill
but simply to teach him to dance

They are peaceful both   these spare
men of Kashmir   and the bear
alive is their living   too
If   far on the Delhi way
around him galvanic they dance
it is merely to wear   wear
from his shaggy body the tranced
wish forever to stay
only an ambling bear
four-footed in berries

It is no more joyous for them
in this hot dust to prance
out of reach of the praying claws
sharpened to paw for ants
in the shadows of deodars[1]

It is not easy to free
myth from reality
or rear this fellow up
to lurch   lurch with them
in the tranced dancing of men

GLOSSARY
1 *deodars*: Himalayan cedars.

EL GRECO:[1] *ESPOLIO*

The carpenter is intent on the pressure of his hand

on the awl   and the trick of pinpointing his strength
through the awl to the wood   which is tough
He has no effort to spare for despoilings
or to worry if he'll be cut in on the dice
His skill is vital to the scene   and the safety of the state
Anyone can perform the indignities   It's his hard arms
and craft that hold the eyes of the convict's women
There is the problem of getting the holes exact
(in the middle of this elbowing crowd)
and deep enough to hold the spikes
after they've sunk through those bared feet
and inadequate wrists he knows are waiting behind him

He doesn't sense perhaps that one of the hands
is held in a curious gesture over him –
giving   or asking   forgiveness? –
but he'd scarcely take time to be puzzled by poses
Criminals come in all sorts   as anyone knows who makes crosses
are as mad or sane as those who decide on their killings
Our one at least has been quiet so far
though they say he talked himself into this trouble
a carpenter's son who got notions of preaching

Well here's a carpenter's son who'll have carpenter sons
God willing   and build what's wanted   temples or tables
mangers or crosses   and shape them decently
working alone in that firm and profound abstraction
which blots out the bawling of rag-snatchers
To construct with hands   knee-weight   braced thigh
keeps the back turned from death

But it's too late now for the other carpenter's boy
to return to this peace before the nails are hammered

GLOSSARY
1 *El Greco*: a Greek painter (1541–1614) who worked in Spain. His painting *Espolio* (*The Disrobing of Christ*) shows the crowd taking off Christ's robe while a carpenter in the foreground of the picture is making a hole in the cross on which Christ is to be crucified.

For George Lamming[1]

To you
    I can risk words about this

Mastering them   you know
    they are dull
        servants
who say less
    and worse
        than we feel

That party above Kingston Town[2]
    we stood   five (six?) couples

linked singing
    more than rum happy

I was giddy
    from sudden friendship
wanted   undeserved

    black tulip faces

self swaying forgotten

    laughter in dance

Suddenly on a wall mirror
    my face assaulted me
stunned to see itself
    like a white snail
        in the supple dark flowers

Always now I move grateful
    to all of you
who let me walk thoughtless
    and unchallenged
in the gardens
    in the castles
        of your skins

GLOSSARY
1 *George Lamming*: a Barbadian writer. His first and best-known novel is *In the Castle of My Skin*, which is about a boy called G growing up in a village in Barbados.
2 *Kingston*: the capital of Jamaica, where Birney wrote this poem in 1962.

TRANSISTOR

She clung to the broom
a long witchy affair she'd been using
to swipe the ancient floor
of the one habitable room
when we came in for a breather
out of the jeep and the humid morning
to this mountain guesthouse
where no one stayed any more
Eyes too bright black to be plumbed
gleamed above the homemade handle
she was just tall enough to see over
and her arms   from the grip of the hands
were torsioned as burnt tree-roots

'Like she was hol'in a mike'
the engineer's little black steno[1] said
and giggled   drifting then to the porch
where her boy friend already had vanished
They had come along for the ride

But the old woman was belting songs out
as if she had to send them all the way
back to the sea and the canebrakes[2]
her greatgrandfather ran from
the night he brought her words
stored in his rebellious head
beyond the howl of the slavers' hounds
to this remotest hilltop in Jamaica

In truth she'd never faced mike nor tape
Today was the first she'd seen a transistor
and she'd stared at that more with fear
than interest   when the little steno
had sauntered by from the jeep with it

An anchor to keep the rest of her tiny self
from floating up level with the notes
was more what she needed the broom for
I thought   utterly stilled in my chair
under the clean power
coiled in four generations of skulls
and springing out now
from the mouth of this bird-still body

It was the engineer she sang for
because he had asked her   he always did
Yet mine was a new face
with the colour to make anyone wary
up in these mountains
So she stood poised for reversal
back to the caretaker's role
But she soon forgot me   him too
as her mind unravelled to airs
a grandmother might have woven
stooping in dappled coffee groves
when this was a plantation house
buzzing with brief whiteman's prospering

She paused only once   to down a glass
the engineer poured from the rum he'd brought
He knew what songs to ask for
and out they came now whorling
as if her voice were immortal and separate
within her   and she only the toughened reed
vibrated still by the singing dead
by the slaved and the half-free
The narrow high-ceilinged room was a box
resounding with all the mourning of loves
and deaths   the fear of Mamba[3]   hope of Jesus
the bitter years and the bawdy
till suddenly   at her first falter
she seemed to listen
and stopped

It was not quite all
though my thanks alone might have sent her off
if the engineer hadn't silently offered
a second rum   The besom[4] again in one hand
like a rifle at ease   she swung to me
and in the grave high rhythms of the Victorians
toasted my health
and that of all the gentlemen of my nation
with all the dignity of hers
then disappeared into her kitchen
broom already waggling

It was only then I let my ear tell me
there'd been a counter bass going on all along
Out on the dusty porch I found the young pair
sitting on the rail at the farthest corner
Two faces   black and anxious

leant together under the transistor
They'd found a nail in a pillar to hang it by
The morning disc spin from Puerto Rico
was sending a Hollywood cowboy
from last year's Parade
The machine swung his voice from shriek
to silence   and back

I suppose they'd been listening to him
as exclusively as I to her
and out of just as much need
to exchange our pasts

GLOSSARY
1 *steno*: stenographer, secretary.
2 *canebrakes*: tracts of land overgrown with cane (sugar-cane).
3 *Mamba*: a Haitian voodoo deity.
4 *besom*: broom.

MEETING OF STRANGERS[1]

'Nice jacket you got dere, man'

He swerved his bicycle toward my curb
to call   then flashed round the corner
a blur in the dusk   of somebody big
redshirted   young   dark   unsmiling

As I stood hoping for a taxi to show
I thought him droll at least
A passing pleasantry?   It was frayed
a sixdollar coat   tropical weight
in this heat only something with pockets
to carry things in

Now all four streets were empty
Dockland   everything shut

It was a sound no bigger than a breath
that made me wheel

He was ten feet away   redshirt
The cycle leant by a post farther off
where an alley came in   What?!

My turning froze him
in the middle of some elaborate stealth
He looked almost comic   splayed
but there was a glitter
under the downheld hand
and something smoked from his eyes

By God if I was going to be stabbed
for my wallet (adrenalin suffused me)
it would have to be done in plain sight
I made a flying leap
to the middle of the crossing
White man   tourist   surrogate   yes
but not guilty enough
to be skewered in the guts for it
without raising all Trinidad first
with shouts   fists   feet   whatever
– I squared round to meet him
and there was a beautiful taxi
lumbering in from a sidestreet
empty!

As I rolled away   safe as Elijah[2]
lucky as Ganymede[3]
there on the curb I'd leaped from
stood that damned cyclist solemnly
shouting

'What did he say?' I asked the driver
He shrugged at the windshield
'Man dat a crazy boogoo[4]
He soun like he say
"dat a nice jump you got too" '

GLOSSARY
1 The poem was written in Port of Spain, Trinidad.
2 *Elijah*: a Hebrew prophet carried to Heaven by a chariot of fire.
3 *Ganymede*: a Greek youth carried to Heaven by an eagle at the command of Zeus.
4 *boogoo*: a word common in Jamaica and Trinidad, used to describe a worthless or ugly person.

LETTER TO A CUZCO PRIEST

Father   whose name
your smalltown paper took in vain

Young father   whose face
blurred in the cheap newsprint
I could not recognize in a street

Father   who will never know me
nor read this   which is written
in your honour
in the terms of my worship

Father   forgive yourself

    This morning two Incas
    tramped on their horny feet
    down sun-ravaged slopes
    clutching cardboard banners
    Thirty more Indians followed
    sunfaced   silent   ragged
    and as many boneknobbly goats
    maybe a hundred sheep
    gut-swollen   yammering
    Their dust rose   was carried
    by thin winds like incense
    over sculptured rocks
    that once bore up the Moon's Temple
    Dry wail of the beasts
    dropping over denuded terraces
    enchanted the ears of travellers
    lining up two Cuzco kids
    (dressed like Inca princelings
    by the Oficina de Tourismo)
    to be shot by cameras
    in front of the Bath of the Priestess

Father   worship yourself

    Where stony slopes level
    to unfenced valleys   the sheep
    took over the lead   sniffing grass
    not the boundary stakes

Father you were not with those shepherds
but your Word sent them

>A local watchman for the Lima agent
>for the American banker
>for the Peruvian landowner
>living in Madrid

>phoned the Cuzco cops
>who phoned the army regiment
>quartered locally to handle such jobs

Father   the guilt is not yours
though words that blazed last week
from your pulpit lettered their placards

>The two who bore them are dead

Father   the guilt begins
in the other pulpits and all the places
where no one will say your words

>'The Government is only
>an armed front for fifty Families'

Where no one calls on whatever his country

>'Let the land feed its people'

Father   the guilt is not that you spoke
nor that the poor listened   acted
have come again to defeat

>Twenty of those who followed
>into convenient range of the troops
>tend their own wounds
>in the jail's bullpen

Father   forgive all men if you must
but only in despite of god
and in Man's name

>Their flocks   driven back
>to the spiny heights
>are herded now by the boys and women

Do not forgive your god
who cannot change   being perfect

    Blood dries on the uncropped grass
    The goats eat dust

Father   honour your Man
though he will not honour you
in whatever priestly purgatory
authority muffles you now

    In Cuzco the paper that quoted the sermon
    and printed your face
    today demands death
    for the Red (Indian?) spies in the Andes

Father   gullible and noble
born to be martyred
and to be the worthy instrument
of the martyrdom of the gullible

    I who am not deceived
    by your cold deity

    believe

    for there is no other belief
    in the wild unquenchable God
    flaming within you

Pray to yourself above all for men like me
that we do not quench
the man
in each of us

Takakkaw Falls

Jupiter[1] Thor[2]   how he thunders!
High in his own cloud somewhere
smashes
explodes on her upslant ledges
arcs out foaming
falls fighting –
o roaring cold down-geyser –
falls
falls gyring   flings
rain rainbows like peacock flights
vaulting the valley
His own gale rends him
heads off spray-comets
that hurl from her taut cliff
shreds even his cataract core
juggles it
struggles – holds?
falls
ho
like Woden[3]
Zeus[4]
down
terrible the bolt of him
(writhing past firs
foamdrowned to skeletons)
the hissing iced-nebulae whirl of him
crashes
batters unstayable
batters bullthroated
life-lunging
Ta-
kak-
kaw
batters the brown
throbbing thighs of his mountain

Out of mist meekly the stream

Milk-young he mewls in naked-green moss
bruise-purple boulders
Slickens to slope   pours
silt-turbulent through pine   races

whole to the Yoho   coils
with Columbia   wanders
the ocean tundra   climbs
by sunladders slowly to
storm
glacier
down to the
spawning
thunder

GLOSSARY
1 *Jupiter*: the most senior deity in the Roman pantheon of gods and goddesses.
2 *Thor*: the god of Thunder, son of Odin in Norse mythology.
3 *Woden*: the old English name for Odin.
4 *Zeus*: the greatest of the Greek gods. The Roman Jupiter is a version of Zeus.

SUGGESTIONS FOR WRITING AND DISCUSSION

1 *Describe the way Birney lays out his poems on the page and comment on the effectiveness of his use of punctuation and typography.*
2 *Choose two of Birney's poems that show his sympathy for people of other countries and races and write about them: for instance, 'Letter to a Cuzco Priest' and 'The Bear on the Delhi Road'.*
3 *Consider the advantages to a poet of using free verse, using two or three of Birney's poems as illustrations and examples.*
4 *Write an account of one of the poems by Birney that has impressed you.*
5 *Describe the different impressions of Caribbean life and people that Birney gives in 'For George Lamming', 'Transistor' and 'Meeting of Strangers'.*
6   *... the clean power*
     coiled in four generations of skulls
     and springing out now
     from the mouth of this bird-still body
The old lady in 'Transistor' is singing songs learnt from her parents and grandparents. See whether you can collect rhymes, songs, or simply 'memories' from your own parents or grandparents. You could group your material under headings such as (a) Historical rhymes or songs, (b) Humorous rhymes or songs, (c) Love songs, and so on.

FURTHER READING

Collected Poems Earle Birney (McClelland & Stewart)
Selected Poems e. e. cummings (Faber)
The Oxford Book of Canadian Verse (Oxford University Press)

JUDITH WRIGHT

Judith Wright was born in 1915 in Armidale, New South Wales, Australia, where her family had a sheep station. She studied at Sydney University and worked as a secretary, clerk, statistician and more recently as a university tutor at the University of Queensland, Brisbane. Her first collection of poems was published in 1946 and she has published a number of collections since then. She is regarded as one of Australia's foremost poets and is also a respected writer on Australian literature. Judith Wright was married to the Australian philosopher the late P. H. McKinney. She has one daughter.

Wright is very much an Australian poet. She writes about people and creatures as seen within the framework of

Australia's landscape and history. She is a very personal poet, but at the same time the incidents she writes about take on a universal and symbolic significance. She reveals a particular intuitive insight into the lives and sensitivities of birds and animals that can be compared with that of the English poet Ted Hughes. She is also conscious of her role as a woman poet, and a number of her poems, particularly in her collection *Woman to Man*, express the poetic vision of a woman as opposed to the predominant male vision.

BULLOCKY

Beside his heavy-shouldered team,
thirsty with drought and chilled with rain,
he weathered all the striding years
till they ran widdershins in his brain:[1]

Till the long solitary tracks
etched deeper with each lurching load
were populous before his eyes,
and fiends and angels used his road.

All the long straining journey grew
a mad apocalyptic dream,
and he old Moses, and the slaves
his suffering and stubborn team.

Then in his evening camp beneath
the half-light pillars of the trees
he filled the steepled cone of night
with shouted prayers and prophecies.

While past the campfire's crimson ring
the star-struck darkness cupped him round,
and centuries of cattlebells
rang with their sweet uneasy sound.

Grass is across the waggon-tracks,
and plough strikes bone beneath the grass,
and vineyards cover all the slopes
where the dead teams were used to pass.

O vine, grow close upon that bone
and hold it with your rooted hand.
The prophet Moses feeds the grape,
and fruitful is the Promised Land.

GLOSSARY
1 *ran widdershins in his brain*: went in the opposite direction to the usual one; went
the wrong way in his mind.

BROTHER AND SISTERS

The road turned out to be a cul-de-sac;
stopped like a lost intention at the gate
and never crossed the mountains to the coast.
But they stayed on. Years grew like grass and leaves
across the half-erased and dubious track
until one day they knew the plans were lost,
the blue-print for the bridge was out of date,
and now their orchards never would be planted.
The saplings sprouted slyly; day by day
the bush moved one step nearer, wondering when.
The polished parlour grew distrait and haunted
where Millie, Lucy, John each night at ten
wound the gilt clock that leaked the year away.

The pianola – oh, listen to the mocking-bird –
wavers on Sundays and has lost a note.
The wrinkled ewes snatch pansies through the fence
and stare with shallow eyes into the garden
where Lucy shrivels waiting for a word,
and Millie's cameos loosen round her throat.
The bush comes near, the ranges grow immense.

Feeding the lambs deserted in early spring
Lucy looked up and saw the stockman's eye
telling her she was cracked and old.
                                    The wall
groans in the night and settles more awry.
O how they lie awake. Their thoughts go fluttering
from room to room like moths: 'Millie, are you awake?'
'Oh John, I have been dreaming.' 'Lucy, do you cry?'
– meet tentative as moths. Antennae stroke a wing.
'There is nothing to be afraid of. Nothing at all.'

THE KILLER

The day was clear as fire,
the birds sang frail as glass,
when thirsty I came to the creek
and fell by its side in the grass.

My breast on the bright moss
and shower-embroidered weeds,
my lips to the live water
I saw him turn in the reeds.

Black horror sprang from the dark
in a violent birth,
and through its cloth of grass
I felt the clutch of earth.

O beat him into the ground.
O strike him till he dies,
or else your life itself
drains through those colourless eyes.

I struck again and again.
Slender in black and red
he lies, and his icy glance
turns outward, clear and dead.

But nimble my enemy
as water is, or wind.
He has slipped from his death aside
and vanished into my mind.

He has vanished whence he came,
my nimble enemy;
and the ants come out to the snake
and drink at his shallow eye.

WOMAN TO CHILD

You who were darkness warmed my flesh
where out of darkness rose the seed.
Then all a world I made in me;
all the world you hear and see
hung upon my dreaming blood.

There moved the multitudinous stars,
and coloured birds and fishes moved.
There swam the sliding continents.
All time lay rolled in me, and sense,
and love that knew not its beloved.

O node and focus of the world;
I hold you deep within that well
you shall escape and not escape –
that mirrors still your sleeping shape;
that nurtures still your crescent cell.

I wither and you break from me;
yet though you dance in living light
I am the earth, I am the root,
I am the stem that fed the fruit,
the link that joins you to the night.

OLD MAN

Before the coming of that arrogant and ancient kingdom
something is waiting to be done, something should be said.
The very old man has lost the clues that led
into the country of his mind, its people are all dead.
He stumbles through the days of bright and sorrowful winter.

The stubble of the corn is raked together and burning
with a sweet smoke that brings a memory to his mind.
He stands on the ploughed earth's edge where the smoke lifts on the wind,
red flame on red earth beckons, but his eyes are blind;
and rocketing up the high wind, magpies are singing.

There is something to be said yet, a word that might be spoken
before the flames blacken and the field is sown again.
Blade and weed will grow over it after the spring rain,
weed and worm will riot in the country of the brain,
but now in the wind on the bared field a word crouches in the open.

Catching at the turns of smoke where the breeze wanders
he leans on the fence, the old old man gone queer,
waiting for the word or his death to come near.
If he can catch either of them, his eyes will suddenly clear –
but the figureless smoke moves on like mist over windows.

Put up the hare, good dog, in a fury of yelling.
Let the red field and the red flame open to watch you run
violent in your intent to the smoky winter sun.
Put up the hare, good dog; catch him before he is gone –
the last hare on the place, perhaps, there's no telling.

But the winter wind brings ice to fill the sky with winter,
and the hare crouches and eludes and the smoke turns aside.
The old man coughs in the eddies, forgetful and red-eyed;
there is no clue to his mind now and all his friends have died.
He must wait for the coming of that arrogant and ancient kingdom.

BIRDS

Whatever the bird is, is perfect in the bird.
Weapon kestrel hard as a blade's curve,
thrush round as a mother or a full drop of water,
fruit-green parrot wise in his shrieking swerve –
all are what bird is and do not reach beyond bird.

Whatever the bird does is right for the bird to do –
cruel kestrel dividing in his hunger the sky,
thrush in the trembling dew beginning to sing,
parrot clinging and quarrelling and veiling his queer eye –
all these are as birds are and good for birds to do.

But I am torn and beleaguered by my own people.
The blood that feeds my heart is the blood they gave me,
and my heart is the house where they gather and fight for dominion –
all different, all with a wish and a will to save me,
to turn me into the ways of other people.

If I could leave their battleground for the forest of a bird
I could melt the past, the present and the future in one
and find the words that lie behind all these languages.
Then I could fuse my passions into one clear stone
and be simple to myself as the bird is to the bird.

THE PEACOCK

Shame on the aldermen who locked
the Peacock in a dirty cage!
His blue and copper sheens are mocked
by habit, hopelessness and age.

The weary Sunday families
along their gravelled paths repeat
the pattern of monotonies
that he treads out with restless feet.

And yet the Peacock shines alone;
and if one metal feather fall
another grows where that was grown.
Love clothes him still, in spite of all.

How pure the hidden spring must rise
that time and custom cannot stain!
It speaks its joy again – again.
Perhaps the aldermen are wise.

WOUNDED NIGHT-BIRD

Walking one lukewarm, lamp-black night I heard
a yard from me his harsh rattle of warning,
and in a landing-net of torchlight saw him crouch –
the devil, small but dangerous. My heart's lurch
betrayed me to myself. But I am learning:
I can distinguish: the devil is no bird.

A bird with a broken breast. But what a stare
he fronted me with – his look abashed my own.
He was all eyes, furious, meant to wound.
And I, who meant to heal, took in my hand
his depth of down, his air-light delicate bone,
his heart in the last extreme of pain and fear.

From nerve to nerve I felt the circuit blaze.
Along my veins his anguish beat; his eyes
flared terror into mine and cancelled time,
and the black whirlpool closed over my head
and clogged my throat with the cry that knows no aid.
Far down beneath the reach of succouring light
we fought, we suffered, we were sunk in night.

THE WAGTAIL

So elegant he is and neat
from round black head to slim black feet!
He sways and flirts upon the fence,
his collar clean as innocence.

The city lady looks and cries
'Oh charming bird with dewdrop eyes,
how kind of you to sing that song!'
But what a pity – she is wrong.

'Sweet-pretty-creature' – yes, but who
is the one he sings it to?
    Not me – not you.

The furry moth, the gnat perhaps,
on which his scissor-beak snip-snaps.

REMEMBERING AN AUNT

Her room was large enough – you would say, private
from the rest of the house, until you looked again
and saw it supervised by her mother's window.
She kept there, face to the wall, some of the pictures
she had once painted; in a cupboard she had carved
was closed some music she had wished to play.

Her hands were pricked and blackened. At the piano
she played the pieces her mother liked to hear –
Chopin and Chaminade, In a Persian Market.
Her smile was awkward. When they said to her,
'Why not take up your sketching again? So pretty—'
she was abrupt. For she remembered Rome,
Florence, the galleries she saw at thirty,
she who had won art prizes at local shows
and played to country women from her childhood.

Brushes, paints, Beethoven put aside
(for ignorant flattery's worse than ignorant blame),
she took her stance and held it till she died.

I praise her for her silence and her pride;
art lay in both. Yet in her, all the same,
sometimes there sprang a small unnoticed flame –
grief too unseen, resentment too denied.

SUGGESTIONS FOR WRITING AND DISCUSSION

1 *Illustrate Judith Wright's skill in portraying animals and birds.*
2 *Many of Judith Wright's poems about people are studies of loneliness and
frustration. Illustrate this by reference to her poems, 'Brother and Sisters'
and 'Remembering an Aunt'.*
3 *What impressions of Australian life and landscape do Judith Wright's
poems give?*
4 *Write an account of one of Judith Wright's poems that has particularly
interested you.*
5 'Bullocky'
*(a) What changes seem to have taken place in the Australian landscape
and way of life since the drover's days?*
*(b) What link does Wright make between Moses and the drover or bul-
locky?*
*(c) What groups of past people, either in the town or in the country, have
contributed to this country's prosperity? Choose one group and write a
short account of them – their work, living conditions, and so on.*
6 *Referring to Wright's 'The Killer' and 'Wounded Night-Bird', note her use
of detail and her use of rhyme. Write your own poem about an unexpected
encounter with a bird or animal.*

FURTHER READING

Collected Poems (1942–70) Judith Wright (Angus & Robertson)
Selected Poems Ted Hughes (Faber)
The Oxford Book of Australian Verse, edited by Judith Wright (Oxford
   University Press)
The Penguin Book of Australian Verse (Penguin)

GABRIEL OKARA

Gabriel Okara was born in the eastern, Delta region of Nigeria in 1921. He attended Government College, Umuahia, and then trained and worked as a bookbinder. Later he moved into publishing and then to the information division of the Nigerian civil service. He began writing poetry in the early 1950s and until the publication of his experimental novel *The Voice*, in 1964, he was known primarily as a poet. In the late 1950s he studied journalism at Northwestern University in the United States. Okara supported Biafra during the Nigerian civil war (1967–70) and in 1969 toured America with the writer Chinua Achebe, putting the case for Biafra. After the war he founded and managed the Rivers State government newspaper *The Nigerian Tide*. He is now head of Rivers State

Cultural Centre. In spite of his having had his poems published in magazines and anthologies since the early 1950s, Okara's first collection of poems did not appear until 1978. Many of his poems were lost in the chaos and destruction of the Nigerian civil war and so were the manuscripts of two novels. He is considered to have written some of the finest war poems on the 1967–70 conflict.

Okara's poetry reflects his deep interest in the literature, language and culture of his people. Often in his poems there is a conflict between the traditional past and the effects of Westernization. He is a reflective poet and makes great use of symbols and imagery to carry his meaning.

ONCE UPON A TIME

Once upon a time, son,
they used to laugh with their hearts
and laugh with their eyes;
but now they only laugh with their teeth,
while their ice-block-cold eyes
search behind my shadow.

There was a time indeed
they used to shake hands with their hearts;
but that's gone, son.
Now they shake hands without hearts
while their left hands search
my empty pockets.

'Feel at home'! 'Come again';
they say, and when I come
again and feel
at home, once, twice,
there will be no thrice –
for then I find doors shut on me.

So I have learned many things, son.
I have learned to wear many faces
like dresses – homeface,
officeface, streetface, hostface,
cocktailface, with all their conforming smiles
like a fixed portrait smile.

And I have learned, too,
to laugh with only my teeth
and shake hands without my heart.
I have also learned to say, 'Goodbye',
when I mean 'Good-riddance';
to say 'Glad to meet you',
without being glad; and to say 'It's been
nice talking to you', after being bored.

But believe me, son.
I want to be what I used to be
when I was like you. I want
to unlearn all these muting things.
Most of all, I want to relearn
how to laugh, for my laugh in the mirror
shows only my teeth like a snake's bare fangs!

So show me, son,
how to laugh; show me how
I used to laugh and smile
once upon a time when I was like you.

PIANO AND DRUMS[1]

When at break of day at a riverside
I hear jungle drums telegraphing
the mystic rhythm, urgent, raw
like bleeding flesh, speaking of
primal youth and the beginning,
I see the panther ready to pounce,
the leopard snarling about to leap
and the hunters crouch with spears poised;

And my blood ripples, turns torrent,
topples the years and at once I'm
in my mother's lap a suckling;
at once I'm walking simple
paths with no innovations,
rugged, fashioned with the naked
warmth of hurrying feet and groping hearts
in green leaves and wild flowers pulsing.

Then I hear a wailing piano
solo speaking of complex ways
in tear-furrowed concerto;
of far-away lands
and new horizons with
coaxing diminuendo, counterpoint,
crescendo. But lost in the labyrinth
of its complexities, it ends in the middle
of a phrase at a daggerpoint.

And I lost in the morning mist
of an age at a riverside keep
wandering in the mystic rhythm
of jungle drums and the concerto.

GLOSSARY
1 The piano symbolizes Western culture. The drums stand for traditional African
culture.

SPIRIT OF THE WIND

The storks are coming now –
white specks in the silent sky.
They had gone north seeking
fairer climes to build their homes
when here was raining.

They are back with me now –
Spirits of the wind,
beyond the gods' confining
hands they go north and west and east,
instinct guiding.

But willed by the gods
I'm sitting on this rock
watching them come and go
from sunrise to sundown, with the spirit
urging within.

And urging a red pool stirs,
and each ripple is
the instinct's vital call,
a desire in a million cells
confined.

O God of the gods and me,
shall I not heed
this prayer-bell call, the moon
angelus, because my stork is caged
in Singed Hair and Dark Skin?

NEW YEAR'S EVE MIDNIGHT

Now the bells are tolling –
A year is dead.
And my heart is slowly beating
the Nunc Dimittis[1]
to all my hopes and mute
yearnings of a year
and ghosts hover round
dream beyond dream

Dream beyond dream
mingling with the dying
bell-sounds fading
into memories
like rain drops
falling into a river.

And now the bells are chiming –
A year is born.
And my heart-bell is ringing
in a dawn.
But it's shrouded things I see
dimly stride
on heart-canopied paths
to a riverside.

GLOSSARY
1 *Nunc Dimittis*: the prayer of Simeon in Luke 2: 29–32: 'Lord, now let me depart in peace.'

YOU LAUGHED AND LAUGHED AND LAUGHED

In your ears my song
is motor car misfiring
stopping with a choking cough;
and you laughed and laughed and laughed.

In your eyes my ante-
natal walk was inhuman, passing
your 'omnivorous understanding'
and you laughed and laughed and laughed.

You laughed at my song,
you laughed at my walk.

Then I danced my magic dance
to the rhythm of talking drums pleading, but you shut your
eyes and laughed and laughed and laughed.

And then I opened my mystic
inside wide like
the sky, instead you entered your
car and laughed and laughed and laughed.

You laughed at my dance,
you laughed at my inside.

You laughed and laughed and laughed.
But your laughter was ice-block
laughter and it froze your inside froze
your voice froze your ears
froze your eyes and froze your tongue.

And now it's my turn to laugh;
but my laughter is not
ice-block laughter. For I
know not cars, know not ice-blocks.

My laughter is the fire
of the eye of the sky, the fire
of the earth, the fire of the air,
the fire of the seas and the
rivers fishes animals trees
and it thawed your inside,
thawed your voice, thawed your
ears, thawed your eyes and
thawed your tongue.

So a meek wonder held
your shadow and you whispered:
'Why so?'
And I answered:
'Because my fathers and I
are owned by the living
warmth of the earth
through our naked feet.'

THE MYSTIC DRUM

The mystic drum beat in my inside
and fishes danced in the rivers
and men and women danced on land
to the rhythm of my drum

But standing behind a tree
with leaves around her waist
she only smiled with a shake of her head.

Still my drum continued to beat,
rippling the air with quickened
tempo compelling the quick
and the dead to dance and sing
with their shadows –

But standing behind a tree
with leaves around her waist
she only smiled with a shake of her head.

Then the drum beat with the rhythm
of the things of the ground
and invoked the eye of the sky
the sun and the moon and the river gods –
and the trees began to dance,
the fishes turned men
and men turned fishes
and things stopped to grow –

But standing behind a tree
with leaves around her waist
she only smiled with a shake of her head.

And then the mystic drum
in my inside stopped to beat –
and men became men,
fishes became fishes
and trees, the sun and the moon
found their places, and the dead
went to the ground and things began to grow.

And behind the tree she stood
with roots sprouting from her
feet and leaves growing on her head
and smoke issuing from her nose
and her lips parted in her smile
turned cavity belching darkness.

Then, then I packed my mystic drum
and turned away; never to beat so loud any more.

THE SNOWFLAKES SAIL GENTLY DOWN[1]

The snowflakes sail gently
down from the misty eye of the sky
and fall lightly on the
winter-weary elms. And the branches
winter-stripped and nude, slowly
with the weight of the weightless snow
bow like grief-stricken mourners
as white funeral cloth is slowly
unrolled over deathless earth.
And dead sleep stealthily from the
heater rose and closed my eyes with
the touch of silk cotton on water falling.

Then I dreamed a dream
in my dead sleep. But I dreamed
not of earth dying and elms a vigil
keeping. I dreamed of birds, black
birds flying in my inside,[2] nesting
and hatching on oil palms bearing suns
for fruits and with roots denting the
uprooters' spades. And I dreamed the
uprooters tired and limp, leaning on my roots –
their abandoned roots
and the oil palms gave them each a sun.

But on their palms
they balanced the blinding orbs
and frowned with schisms on their
brows – for the suns reached not
the brightness of gold!

Then I awoke. I awoke
to the silently falling snow
and bent-backed elms bowing and
swaying to the winter wind like
white-robed Moslems salaaming[3] at evening
prayer, and the earth lying inscrutable
like the face of a god in a shrine.

GLOSSARY
1 This poem was inspired by the poet's first experience of snow while studying in the United States.
2 *inside*: here this is a translation of an expression from Okara's mother-tongue, Ijo. He uses it frequently in his writing and for him it represents the sum total of the human being.
3 *salaaming*: bowing in prayer.

SUDDENLY THE AIR CRACKS

Suddenly the air cracks
with striking cracking rockets
guffaw of bofors[1] stuttering LMGs[2]
jets diving shooting glasses dropping
breaking from lips people diving
under beds nothing bullets flashing fire
striking writhing bodies and walls –

Suddenly there's silence –
And a thick black smoke
rises sadly into the sky as the jets
fly away in gruesome glee –

Then a babel of emotions, voices
mothers fathers calling children
and others joking shouting 'where's your bunker?'
laughing teasing across streets
and then they gaze in groups without sadness
at the sad smoke curling skywards –

Again suddenly, the air cracks
above rooftops cracking striking
rockets guffawing bofors stuttering LMGs
ack ack[3] flacks diving jets
diving men women dragging children
seeking shelter not there breathless
hugging gutters walls houses
crumbling rumbling thunder
bombs hearts thumping heads low
under beds moving wordless lips –

Then suddenly there's silence –
and the town heaves a deep sigh
as the jets again fly away and the guns
one by one fall silent and the gunners
dazed gaze at the empty sky, helpless –

And then voices shouting calling
voices, admiring jet's dive
pilots' bravery blaming gunners
praising gunners laughing people
wiping sweat and dust from hair
neck and shirt with trembling hands.

Things soon simmer to normal
hum and rhythm as danger passes
and the streets are peopled
with strolling men and women
boys and girls on various errands
walking talking laughing smiling –
and children running with arms
stretched out in front playing
at diving jets zoom past
unsmiling bombing rocketing shooting
with mouths between startled feet.

This also passes as dusk descends
and a friendly crescent moon
appears where the jets were.
Then simmering silence – the day passes –
And the curling black smoke,
the sadless hearts and the mangled
bodies stacked in the morgue
become memorials of this day.

GLOSSARY
1 *bofors*: light anti-aircraft guns.
2 *LMGs*: light machine-guns.
3 *ack ack*: imitative name for light machine-guns.

SUGGESTIONS FOR WRITING AND DISCUSSION

1 *Choose two of Okara's poems that describe conflicts of feelings or attitudes and explain the conflicts.*
2 *Write a critical account of* 'Piano and Drums' *or* 'Suddenly the Air Cracks'. *(In* 'Piano and Drums' *mention the contrasting images used and the way the poem resolves the conflict; in* 'Suddenly the Air Cracks' *mention the detail used in the different scenes and the use of techniques such as alliteration.)*
3 *Select some of the symbols and images Okara uses and explain their effectiveness.*
4 *Give an account of the elements in Okara's poetry which strike you as being particularly 'African'. You could refer to the content of the poems, the images and symbols used, and features of style such as repetition.*
5 *'You Laughed and Laughed and Laughed'. Point out the effect of the contrasting images of ice and fire. What are the basic differences between the speaker and the person he is addressing?*
6 *'The Snowflakes Sail Gently Down'*
  (a) What characteristics of winter does Okara stress in the first stanza?
  (b) How do you interpret the 'black birds' and 'the oil palms bearing suns for fruits'?
  (c) What besides the weather has changed when the poet wakes up?
7 *Imagine you are one of the people present in the scenes described in* 'Suddenly the Air Cracks' *and give your version of events. Alternatively, ask someone who has had experience of combat to describe the events to you. Write up his or her account.*

FURTHER READING

The Fisherman's Invocation Gabriel Okara (Heinemann Educational Books)
Idanre Wole Soyinka (Eyre Methuen)
Labyrinths with Path of Thunder Christopher Okigbo (Heinemann Educational Books)
Casualties John Pepper Clark (Longman)
Poems of Black Africa, edited by Wole Soyinka (Heinemann Educational Books)

DENNIS BRUTUS

Dennis Brutus was born in Salisbury, Rhodesia (now Zimbabwe), in 1924, of South African parents of mixed race. While Brutus was a child his family returned to South Africa. He graduated from Fort Hare University and taught English and Afrikaans in Port Elizabeth. He was dismissed and imprisoned for his stand against racism and the apartheid laws of South Africa. As president of SANROC (South Africa Non-Racial Olympic Committee) he was largely responsible for South Africa and Rhodesia being excluded from the Olympic Games. He was arrested and served a prison sentence on Robben Island. After living for a short period in London he moved to the United States and is now Professor of English at Northwestern University.

Brutus has written many poems about his imprisonment and about the horrors of the regime in South Africa. At the same time, his poems express love for the country he lived in. His language and versification are simple and direct. If anything, the hardship and suffering are understated, with the result that the experiences described are conveyed with even greater force.

The five poems from the sequence *Letters to Martha* express aspects of the strains of life under an oppressive regime.

> 'The not-knowing'
> 'It is not all terror'
> 'Quite early one reaches a
>   stage'
> 'In prison'
> 'I remember rising one
>   night'

These poems all describe Brutus's experiences as a political prisoner on Robben Island. On release from prison, he was forbidden to write anything for publication. These poems were written as 'letters' to his sister-in-law Martha after his brother had been sent to Robben Island.

In ' "It is the constant image of your face" ', Brutus writes about the conflict between personal love and love for one's country. 'For a Dead African' praises the brave dead and looks forward to the liberation of his country. The final poem, ' "I am the tree" ', is one of a set of four poems written to mark South African Freedom Day, 26 June 1967. This sets out three different images of suffering and protest. The images are specific to South Africa yet at the same time universal.

'COLD'

the clammy cement
sucks our naked feet

a rheumy yellow bulb
lights a damp grey wall

the stubbled grass
wet with three o'clock dew
is black with glittery edges;

we sit on the concrete,
stuff with our fingers
the sugarless pap
into our mouths

then labour erect;

form lines;

steel ourselves into fortitude
or accept an image of ourselves
numb with resigned acceptance;

the grizzled senior warder comments:
'Things like these
I have no time for;

they are worse than rats;
you can only shoot them.'

Overhead
the large frosty glitter of the stars
the Southern Cross flowering low;

the chains on our ankles
and wrists
that pair us together
jangle

glitter.

We begin to move
    awkwardly.

(Colesberg: en route to Robben Island)

FROM LETTERS TO MARTHA

9

The not-knowing
is perhaps the worst part of the agony
for those outside;

not knowing what cruelties must be endured
what indignities the sensitive spirit must face
what wounds the mind can be made to inflict on itself;

and the hunger to be thought of
to be remembered
and to reach across space
with filaments of tenderness
and consolation.

And knowledge,
even when it is knowledge of ugliness
seems to be preferable,
can be better endured.

And so,
for your consolation
I send these fragments,
random pebbles I pick up
from the landscape of my own experience,
traversing the same arid wastes
in a montage of glimpses
I allow myself
or stumble across.

10

It is not all terror
and deprivation,
you know;

one comes to welcome the closer contact
and understanding one achieves
with one's fellow-men,
fellows, compeers;

and the discipline does much to force
a shape and pattern on one's daily life
as well as on the days

and honest toil
offers some redeeming hours
for the wasted years;

so there are times
when the mind is bright and restful
though alive:
rather like the full calm morning sea.

16

Quite early one reaches a stage
where one resolves to embrace
the status of prisoner
with all it entails,
savouring to the full its bitterness
and seeking to escape nothing:

'Mister,
this is prison;
just get used to the idea'

'You're a convict now.'

Later one changes,
tries the dodges,
seeks the easy outs.

But the acceptance
once made
deep down
remains.

17

In prison
the clouds assume importance
and the birds

With a small space of sky
cut off by walls
of bleak hostility
and pressed upon by hostile authority
the mind turns upwards
when it can –

– there can be no hope
of seeing the stars:
the arcs and fluorescents
have blotted them out –

the complex aeronautics
of the birds
and their exuberant acrobatics
become matters for intrigued speculation
and wonderment

clichés about the freedom of the birds
and their absolute freedom from care
become meaningful

and the graceful unimpeded motion of the clouds
– a kind of music, poetry, dance –
sends delicate rhythms tremoring through the flesh
and fantasies course easily through the mind:
– where are they going
where will they dissolve
will they be seen by those at home
and whom will they delight?

18

I remember rising one night
after midnight
and moving
through an impulse of loneliness
to try and find the stars.

And through the haze
the battens of fluorescents made
I saw pinpricks of white
I thought were stars.

Greatly daring
I thrust my arm through the bars
and easing the switch in the corridor
plunged my cell in darkness

I scampered to the window
and saw the splashes of light
where the stars flowered.

But through my delight
thudded the anxious boots
and a warning barked
from the machine-gun post
on the catwalk.

And it is the brusque inquiry
and threat
that I remember of that night
rather than the stars.

'Somehow we survive'

Somehow we survive
and tenderness, frustrated, does not wither.

Investigating searchlights rake
our naked unprotected contours;

over our heads the monolithic decalogue
of fascist prohibition glowers
and teeters for a catastrophic fall;

boots club the peeling door.

But somehow we survive
severance, deprivation, loss.

Patrols uncoil along the asphalt dark
hissing their menace to our lives,

most cruel, all our land is scarred with terror,
rendered unlovely and unlovable;
sundered are we and all our passionate surrender

but somehow tenderness survives.

Nightsong: City

Sleep well, my love, sleep well:
the harbour lights glaze over restless docks,
police cars cockroach through the tunnel streets;

from the shanties' creaking iron-sheets
violence like a bug-infested rag is tossed
and fear is immanent as sound in the wind-swung bell;

the long day's anger pants from sand and rocks;
but for this breathing night at least,
my land, my love, sleep well.

'IT IS THE CONSTANT IMAGE OF YOUR FACE'

It is the constant image of your face
framed in my hands as you knelt before my chair
the grave attention of your eyes
surveying me amid my world of knives
that stays with me, perennially accuses
and convicts me of heart's-treachery;
and neither you nor I can plead excuses
for you, you know, can claim no loyalty –
my land takes precedence of all my loves.

Yet I beg mitigation, pleading guilty
for you, my dear, accomplice of my heart
made, without words, such blackmail with your beauty
and proffered me such dear protectiveness
that I confess without remorse or shame
my still-fresh treason to my country
and hope that she, my other, dearest love
will pardon freely, not attaching blame
being your mistress (or your match) in tenderness.

FOR A DEAD AFRICAN

We have no heroes and no wars
only victims of a sickly state
succumbing to the variegated sores
that flower under lashing rains of hate.

We have no battles and no fights
for history to record with trite remark
only captives killed on eyeless nights
and accidental dyings in the dark.

Yet when the roll of those who died
to free our land is called, without surprise
these nameless unarmed ones will stand beside
the warriors who secured the final prize.

[*John Nangoza Jebe: shot by the police in a Good Friday procession in Port Elizabeth 1956*]

'I AM THE TREE'

I am the tree
creaking in the wind
outside in the night
twisted and stubborn:

I am the sheet
of the twisted tin shack
grating in the wind
in a shrill sad protest:

I am the voice
crying in the night
that cries endlessly
and will not be consoled.

SUGGESTIONS FOR WRITING AND DISCUSSION

1 *Read '"Cold"' and 'Letters to Martha' 10, 16, 17 and 18. Either (a) Write your own imaginative account of a day in the kind of prison Brutus is describing, or (b) Write a letter to someone outside. You could write in prose, or use free verse as Brutus does.*

2 *Find out what you can about prison conditions in Britain (or in any other country about which you can obtain information). Write your own short report. In what ways are conditions different from or similar to those which Brutus describes?*

3 *By reference to two or more of the poems here show how Brutus's love for his country is expressed in his poetry.*

4 *Describe the picture of urban life in South Africa given in 'Nightsong: City', '"Somehow we survive"' and '"I am the tree"'. Illustrate the techniques that Brutus uses in these poems.*

5 *'The simplicity with which Brutus speaks is what makes his voice so powerful.' Discuss this statement with reference to some of the poems selected here.*

6 *Write your own poem describing an unpleasant city or town scene. (If necessary you could work from a photograph of a place you do not know.)*

7 *Can poetry sometimes make political statements more effectively than prose? Defend your case with examples from as many sources as possible.*

FURTHER READING

Letters to Martha Dennis Brutus (Heinemann Educational Books)
A Simple Lust Dennis Brutus (Heinemann Educational Books)
Stubborn Hope Dennis Brutus (Heinemann Educational Books)

JAMES K. BAXTER

James K. Baxter was born in Dunedin, New Zealand, in 1926. As a young man, he gave up his university course and led an aimless life of manual jobs and drink – as he himself wrote, the life of 'a hobo'. Later he completed his degree and concentrated on writing and on academic work. In 1958, having earlier joined Alcoholics Anonymous, he became a Roman Catholic. He engaged in social work among drug addicts, alcoholics, the homeless and the unemployed. In 1969 he settled in Jerusalem, a small Maori settlement, having heard 'a call' and set out with only a change of clothes and a Bible in Maori. Thus he became what he described as 'a Christian guru, a barefooted and bearded eccentric, a bad smell in the noses of many good citizens'. He died in 1972.

Baxter was a prolific poet. He spoke very strongly for what might be called the casualties of society. His poems also often express a strong bond of sympathy with unexceptional, ordinary people (as in 'Farmhand', 'Mill Girl' and 'Elegy for an Unknown Soldier'). He was critical of 'the dehumanizing aspects of contemporary culture' and felt deeply 'the gulf which lay between man's ideal of peace and the rigours of living in a hostile world'. The passion with which he held these views is strongly conveyed in his poetry.

ELEGY FOR AN UNKNOWN SOLDIER

There was a time when I would magnify
His ending; scatter words as if I wept
Tears not my own but man's. There was a time.
But not now so. He died of a common sickness.

Nor did any new star shine
Upon that day when he came crying out
Of fleshy darkness to a world of pain
And waxen eyelids let the daylight enter.

So felt and tasted, found earth good enough.
Later he played with stones and wondered
If there was land beyond the dark sea rim
And where the road led out of the farthest paddock.

Awkward at school, he could not master sums.
Could you expect him then to understand
The miracle and menace of his body
That grew as mushrooms grow from dusk to dawn?

He had the weight though for a football scrum
And thought it fine to listen to the cheering
And drink beer with the boys, telling them tall
Stories of girls that he had never known.

So when the War came he was glad and sorry,
But soon enlisted. Then his mother cried
A little, and his father boasted how
He'd let him go, though needed for the farm.

Likely in Egypt he would find out something
About himself, if flies and drunkenness
And deadly heat could tell him much – until
In his first battle a shell splinter caught him.

So crown him with memorial bronze among
The older dead, child of a mountainous island.
Wings of a tarnished victory shadow him
Who born of silence has burned back to silence.

FARMHAND

You will see him light a cigarette
At the hall door careless, leaning his back
Against the wall, or telling some new joke
To a friend, or looking out into the secret night.

But always his eyes turn
To the dance floor and the girls drifting like flowers
Before the music that tears
Slowly in his mind an old wound open.

His red sunburnt face and hairy hands
Were not made for dancing or love-making
But rather the earth wave breaking
To the plough, and crops slow-growing as his mind.

He has no girl to run her fingers through
His sandy hair, and giggle at his side
When Sunday couples walk. Instead
He has his awkward hopes, his envious dreams to yarn to.

But ah in harvest watch him
Forking stooks, effortless and strong –
Or listening like a lover to the song
Clear, without fault, of a new tractor engine.

THE HERMIT

Where the salt creek broadens to a brown lagoon
Fringed with matted swordgrass and sea wrack,
There in a corrugated iron shack
Behind a brushwood fence, he lives alone –
The odd-job man, old bludger, worn-out soak,
Hoeing spuds in his garden on the dune
Or mowing lawns by the summer cribs of townsfolk.

Three children married and a wife dead,
He has little enough to live for, one would say.
In mine and threshing-mill he had his day
Bullocking, a strong back and weak head
(Pipe music, Irish whiskey, quids to spend)
Now lies rheumatic in his stretcher bed
Feeling the raw cold and his nearing end.

The rotten boards are barely weatherproof,
Grey spiders scuttle in the draught and damp.
Late in the evening by his spirit lamp
'I am the Resurrection and the Life'
He reads, thumbing a worn bible page;
And when the kids throw pebbles on his roof
Smiles, and remembers his own sapling age.

Then, as his eyes fail in the growing dusk,
Kneels down upon a sacking rug and prays,
His heart like wax in God's meridian blaze,
His body shaken like a burnt-out husk –
Praises that Love who wakened him to weep
When drawn vertiginous[1] in a deathly masque[2]
By *ignis fatuus*[3] and the smell of sleep.

Morning finds him on his daily round,
Stripping black mussels on a tide-swept ledge
Or clipping fronds from the macrocarpa hedge
That guards some well-fed bookie's house and ground.
And soon a wave will take him, or the cold
March gales, his lean flesh in a sodden mound
His spent soul to that river where none grow old.

GLOSSARY
1 *vertiginous*: giddy, dizzy.
2 *deathly masque*: masked dance of death.
3 *ignis fatuus*: will-o'-the-wisp, i.e. a false light.

MILL GIRL

Attendant angel, mark this one
Fresh as paint in the flower of her sixteenth year:
With sheltering wing surround her. The great loom she
Tends, like a monstrous child – its bellowings stun,
Drug, drown her mind like the drumming of a weir;
Her heart's yet innocent of time's captivity.

Nor does she see behind the eyes that feed
On her rose, rash nubility (the tough boys
Who yarn, mending the broken bobbin-strings)
A tigerish jungle of incontinent need,
A cobra's nonchalance swaying at poise,
A bar room vanity that blinks and springs.

She waits in the ignorant garden of her wishes
Till Mr Right (first glimpsed in *The Oracle*) come
Dark-haired and smiling to take her ungloved hand
And lead her into a world lovely as fishes,
Secret as starlight, out of the stagnant slum
She knows, the flyspecked kitchen, to a table at the Grand.

Though Love cannot save, at least it will watch and weep
On that near night when she, under a moonless sky
On wet park leaves, or on a mattress in a back
Room at the party, loses what none can keep –
Rough and ready, before the keg runs dry
Fumbled and forced – yet willing, ready to learn the knack.

A ROPE FOR HARRY FAT

Oh some have killed in angry love
  And some have killed in hate,
And some have killed in foreign lands
  To serve the business State.
The hangman's hands are abstract hands
  Though sudden death they bring –
'The hangman keeps our country pure,'
  Says Harry Fat the King.

Young love will kick the chairs about
   And like a rush fire burn,
Desiring what it cannot have,
   A true love in return.
Who knows what rage and darkness fall
   When lovers' thoughts grow cold?
'Whoever kills must pay the price,'
   Says Harry Fat the old.

With violent hands a young man tries
   To mend the shape of life.
This one used a shotgun
   And that one used a knife.
And who can see the issues plain
   That vex our groaning dust?
'The Law is greater than the man,'
   Says Harry Fat the just.

Te Whiu was too young to vote,
   The prison records show.
Some thought he was too young to hang;
   Legality said, *No.*
Who knows what fear the raupo hides
   Or where the wild duck flies?
'A trapdoor and a rope is best,'
   Says Harry Fat the wise.

Though many a time he rolled his coat
   And on the bare boards lay,
He lies in heavy concrete now
   Until the Reckoning Day.
In linen sheet or granite aisle
   Sleep Ministers of State.
'We cannot help the idle poor,'
   Says Harry Fat the great.

Mercy stirred like a summer wind
   The wigs and polished boots
And the long Jehovah faces
   Above their Sunday suits.
The jury was uncertain;
   The judge debated long.
'Let Justice take her rightful course,'
   Said Harry Fat the strong.

The butcher boy and baker boy
   Were whistling in the street
When the hangman bound Te Whiu's eyes
   And strapped his hands and feet,
Who stole to buy a bicycle
   And killed in panic blood.
'The parson won his soul at length,'
   Said Harry Fat the good.

Oh some will kill in rage and fear
   And some will kill in hate,
And some will kill in foreign lands
   To serve the master State.
Justice walks heavy in the land;
   She bears a rope and shroud.
'We will not change our policy,'
   Says Harry Fat the proud.

MOTHER CRAWFORD'S BOARDING HOUSE[1]

In Mother Crawford's boarding house the company is grand,
There's bludgers, thieves and con men, who will take you by the hand,
A bloody sight more human than the company outside,
And very very seldom are you taken for a ride.

In Mother Crawford's boarding house the food is extra good,
Though the medical attention is at times a little crude.
I told a bloody demon,[2] though he didn't understand,
I thought their hospitality the finest in the land.

In Mother Crawford's boarding house when metho boys arrive
They lay a great red carpet down and welcome them inside.
There's a pigsty and an orchard where we wander in the sun,
And the screws are always helpful as a father to a son.

In Mother Crawford's boarding house you've time to meditate
Upon the good advice you've had from many a magistrate,
And if you stay a year or two, you needn't do it hard,
The only disadvantage is the fact the door is barred.

1 *Mother Crawford's Boarding House*: gaol.
2 *demon*: prison slang for detective.

THE GUNNER'S LAMENT

(for my wife, Te Kare[1])

A Maori gunner lay dying
In a paddyfield north of Saigon,
And he said to his pakeha[2] cobber,[3]
'I reckon I've had it, man!

'And if I could fly like a bird
To my old granny's whare[4]
A truck and a winch would never drag
Me back to the Army.

'A coat and a cap and a well-paid job
Looked better than shovelling metal,
And they told me that Te Rauparaha[5]
Would have fought in the Vietnam battle.

'On my last leave the town swung round
Like a bucket full of eels.
The girls liked the uniform
And I liked the girls.

'Like a bullock to the abattoirs
In the name of liberty
They flew me with a hangover
Across the Tasman Sea,

'And what I found in Vietnam
Was mud and blood and fire,
With the Yanks and the Reds taking turns
At murdering the poor.

'And I saw the reason for it
In a Viet Cong's blazing eyes –
We fought for the crops of kumara[6]
And they are fighting for rice.

'So go and tell my sweetheart
To get another boy
Who'll cuddle her and marry her
And laugh when the bugles blow.

'And tell my youngest brother
He can have my shotgun
To fire at the ducks on the big lagoon,
But not to aim it at a man.

'And tell my granny to wear black
And carry a willow leaf,
Because the kid she kept from the cold
Has eaten a dead man's loaf,

'And go and tell Keith Holyoake[7]
Sitting in Wellington,
However long he scrubs his hands
He'll never get them clean.'

GLOSSARY
1 *Te Kare*: an object of affection (Maori). Baxter's name for his wife.
2 *pakeha*: New Zealander of European descent.
3 *cobber*: friend (Australian, New Zealand).
4 *whare*: house; pronounced waa-ree.
5 *Te Rauparaha*: Maori warrior and hero.
6 *kumara*: sweet potato.
7 *Keith Holyoake*: Prime Minister of New Zealand (1960–72).

THE SURFMAN'S STORY

On such a day as this
When breakers bay on the reef like a minutegun
    Or up the tall beach grind and hiss
    Like flattened snakes – we hauled out
    Tackle and lifeline, at the run,
For two swept seaward, bathers, caught in the current's rout.

(There by the Maori Rock
A narrow rip runs out, rapid as death,
    Each tide, regular as the clock:
    Nothing to fear, once known – but a few
    Fool bathers drowned there a bad name bequeath
Till it grows to a gorgon myth, a cud for gossips to chew.)

      I stood by the reel
And Jake plunged in a smother of surf and sand.
      He could swim, that boy, like a river-eel;
      It was hard going even for his crawlstroke –
      I cursed the mad bathers, you'll understand.
Over his head the flurry of waves battered and broke.

      He told us after how
They beat him off; or rather the man did (she
      Was near sinking). He warded the blow,
      Trod water, waited; then by the hair
      Hauled her, a dead weight, from the treacherous sea
Back through the hurly-burly of breakers to earth and air.

      We worked for an hour to keep
The spark in her body alive; then gave her rum,
      Wrapt her in blankets to lie and sleep
      In the shed down there (the lupin and swordgrass
      Half hide it). But when she had come
To her senses it was only to yammer and cry *Alas*.

Like a dove that has lost its mate,
Or an eagle maybe (she had more that look
In the full lip and nose knife-straight,
Great cavernous eye): she'd have run back
To the brawling sea if I hadn't took
Her by the arms and held her – the bruises stayed blue-black.

It seemed they had made a pact
To drown together, impatient of Love's slow
Guttering to death, and what life lacked
For two fettered in wedlock, wild
To wound each other – the undertow
Of passion drew them till it seemed the blind sea smiled.

Well – he was washed ashore
Some weeks after, eaten by fishes, foul
With tangleweed. She cried no more.
We were married within the year: that house
By the river's ours, with the climbing cowl
Of woodsmoke, the paddock behind, in a nest of orchard boughs.

SUGGESTIONS FOR WRITING AND DISCUSSION

1 *Using the poems selected here, illustrate Baxter's concern for the less fortunate members of society.*
2 *Choose one of the characters Baxter writes about. Re-tell his or her story in his or her own words.*
3 *'Baxter's poems press with passion the right of each individual to be allowed to live his own life.' Discuss.*
4 *Write an account of one of Baxter's poems that has touched your feelings.*
5 *'A Rope for Harry Fat'*
   (a) What attitudes in society is Baxter criticizing in this poem? What was Te Whiu's crime? Did he deserve to be hanged?
   (b) Set out your arguments and then debate the case for and against capital punishment.
6 *Show by discussing 'Elegy for an Unknown Soldier' and 'The Gunner's Lament' how Baxter can be seen as an anti-war poet.*

FURTHER READING

Collected Poems James K. Baxter (Oxford University Press)
The Penguin Book of New Zealand Verse (Penguin)
The Oxford Book of New Zealand Verse (Oxford University Press)

EDWARD
KAMAU
BRATHWAITE

Edward Kamau Brathwaite was
born in Barbados in 1930. He
was educated there and at
Pembroke College, Cambridge,
where he read history. He spent
some years teaching in Ghana
before returning to become a
lecturer in history at the
University of the West Indies.
His collections of poems include
Rights of Passage, *Masks*,
Islands (later published as a
trilogy, *The Arrivants*) and
Mother Poem.

Brathwaite is much concerned
in his poetry with the history of
his people, going back to their
African origins, the experience
of transportation and slavery
and of more recent migration.
All of this leads him to search for
his own identity as a black man.
Such diverse strands also result
in daring experimentations with
language, sound and rhythm.

His poems tend to be written as long sequences and selecting isolated poems by him can give only a partial impression of his power and range.

Brathwaite is part of the important 'second phase' of West Indian writing through his emphasis on an aesthetic re-awakening and a positive re-assessment of Caribbean identity. He sees the artist as an essentially solitary, creative figure, one who points out with visionary power truths about society and history to the rest of the community. In his poetry, alongside the influence of T. S. Eliot (in, for instance, his use of cultural and historical allusions) runs the conscious use of folk speech patterns and rhythms, and the use of dialect or 'nation language' (a term Brathwaite himself uses). In the words of the critic Michael Dash, dialect in Brathwaite's poetry becomes 'a tool for exploring the Caribbean landscape and is moulded by the poet's creative authority. It is also part of the conscious process of repossession' (in Bruce King, ed., *West Indian Literature*, Macmillan, 1979, p. 226).

The poems here are from two of the three long poems that form the trilogy *The Arrivants* and from a later collection entitled *Other Exiles*.

'The Emigrants' is from Section III of *Rights of Passage* which has the sub-title 'Islands and Exiles'. It depicts the suffering and humiliation of the black 'diaspora' and sets against this a historical image of the beauty and harmony that existed before the arrival of Christopher Columbus. The last section sets out, perhaps a little ironically, possible avenues of protest and action available and names three prominent spokesmen for black rights.

THE EMIGRANTS

1

So you have seen them
with their cardboard grips,
felt hats, rain-
cloaks, the women
with their plain
or purple-tinted
coats hiding their fatten-
ed hips.

These are The Emigrants
On sea-port quays
at air-ports
anywhere where there is ship
or train, swift
motor car, or jet
to travel faster than the breeze
you see them gathered:
passports stamped
their travel papers wrapped
in old disused news-
papers: lining their patient queues.

Where to?
They do not know.
Canada, the Panama
Canal, the Miss-
issippi painfields, Florida?
Or on to dock
at hissing smoke locked
Glasgow?

Why do they go?
They do not know.
Seeking a job
they settle for the very best
the agent has to offer:
jabbing a neighbour
out of work for four bob
less a week.

What do they hope for
what find there
these New World mariners
Columbus coursing kaffirs[1]

What Cathay[2] shores
for them are gleaming golden
what magic keys they carry to unlock
what gold endragoned doors?

2

Columbus from his after-
deck watched stars, absorbed in water,
melt in liquid amber drifting

through my summer air.
Now with morning, shadows lifting,
beaches stretched before him cold and clear.

Birds circled flapping flag and mizzen
mast: birds harshly hawking, without fear.
Discovery he sailed for was so near.

Columbus from his after-
deck watched heights he hoped for,
rocks he dreamed, rise solid from my simple water.

Parrots screamed. Soon he would touch
our land, his charted mind's desire.
The blue sky blessed the morning with its fire.

But did his vision
fashion, as he watched the shore,
the slaughter that his soldiers

furthered here? Pike
point and musket butt,
hot splintered courage, bones

cracked with bullet shot,
tipped black boot in my belly, the
whip's uncurled desire?

Columbus from his after-
deck saw bearded fig trees, yellow pouis[3]
blazed like pollen and thin

waterfalls suspended in the green
as his eyes climbed towards the highest ridges
where our farms were hidden.

Now he was sure
he heard soft voices mocking in the leaves.
What did this journey mean, this

new world mean: dis-
covery? Or a return to terrors
he had sailed from, known before?

I watched him pause.

Then he was splashing silence.
Crabs snapped their claws
and scattered as he walked towards our shore.

3

But now the claws are iron: mouldy
dredges do not care what we discover here:
the Mississippi mud is sticky:

men die there
and bouquets of stench lie
all night long along the river bank.

In London, Undergrounds are cold.
The train rolls in from darkness
with our fears

and leaves a lonely soft metallic clanking
in our ears.
In New York

nights are hot
in Harlem, Brooklyn,
along Long Island Sound

This city is so vast
its ears have ceased to know
a simple human sound

Police cars wail
like babies
an ambulance erupts

like breaking glass
an elevator sighs
like Jews in Europe's gases

then slides us swiftly
down the ropes to hell.
Where is the bell

that used to warn us,
playing cricket on the beach,
that it was mid-day: sun too hot

for heads. And evening's
angelus of fish soup,
prayers, bed?

4

My new boss
has no head
for (female) figures

my lover
has no teeth
does not chew

chicken bones.
Her mother wears
a curly headed wig.

5

Once when we went to Europe, a rich old lady asked:
Have you no language of your own
no way of doing things
did you spend all those holidays
at England's apron strings?

And coming down the Bellevueplatz
a bow-legged workman
said: This country's getting pretty flat
with *nègres en Switzerland.*

6

The chaps who drive the City buses
don't like us clipping for them much;
in fact, make quite a fuss.
Bus strikes loom soon.

The men who lever ale
in stuffy Woodbine pubs
don't like us much.
No drinks there soon.

Or broken bottles.
The women who come down
to open doors a crack
will sometimes crack

your fingers if you don't
watch out. Sorry!
Full! Not even Bread
and Breakfast soon

for curly headed workers.
So what to do, man?
Ban the Bomb? Bomb
the place down?

Boycott the girls?
Put a ban on all
marriages? Call
You'self X[4]

wear a beard
and a turban
washing your tur-
bulent sex

about six
times a day:
going Muslim?
Black as God

brown is good
white as sin?
An' doan forget Jimmy Baldwin[5]
an' Martin Luther King[6] . . .

7

Our colour beats a restless drum
but only the bitter come.

GLOSSARY
1 *Columbus coursing kaffirs*: 'kaffirs' is an insulting term for black people, and here it
  suggests the travels and travails of black people who explore, like Christopher
  Columbus, but unlike him must search the world for new homes in order to survive.
2 *Cathay*: a poetic name for China.
3 *pouis*: large and strong flowering tree, also called the 'Sunshine' tree.
4 *Call You'self X*: like Malcolm X. A protest against bearing the name originally given
  to them by a slave-owner.
5 *Jimmy Baldwin*: James Baldwin, a black US writer.
6 *Martin Luther King*: leader of the US Civil Rights movement.

SOUTH

But today I recapture the islands'
bright beaches: blue mist from the ocean
rolling into the fishermen's houses.
By these shores I was born: sound of the sea
came in at my window, life heaved and breathed in me then
with the strength of that turbulent soil.

Since then I have travelled: moved far from the beaches:
sojourned in stoniest cities, walking the lands of the north
in sharp slanting sleet and the hail,
crossed countless saltless savannas and come
to this house in the forest where the shadows oppress me
and the only water is rain and the tepid taste of the river.

We who are born of the ocean can never seek solace
in rivers: their flowing runs on like our longing,
reproves us our lack of endeavour and purpose,
proves that our striving will founder on that.
We resent them this wisdom, this freedom: passing us
toiling, waiting and watching their cunning declension down to the sea.

But today I would join you, travelling river,
borne down the years of your patientest flowing,
past pains that would wreck us, sorrows arrest us,
hatred that washes us up on the flats;
and moving on through the plains that receive us,
processioned in tumult, come to the sea.

Bright waves splash up from the rocks to refresh us,
blue sea-shells shift in their wake
and *there* is the thatch of the fishermen's houses, the path
made of pebbles, and look!
small urchins combing the beaches
look up from their traps to salute us:

they remember us just as we left them.
The fisherman, hawking the surf on this side
of the reef, stands up in his boat
and halloos us: a starfish lies in its pool.
And gulls, white sails slanted seaward,
fly into the limitless morning before us.

FOOTNOTE
This follows straight on after 'The Emigrants' in the 'Islands and Exiles' section of
Rights of Passage.
　　Ancestors, *Ogun* and *Leopard* are all from Section IV of *Islands*, the third part of the
trilogy. The section is sub-titled 'Possession'.

FROM ANCESTORS

Every Friday morning my grandfather
left his farm of canefields, chickens, cows,
and rattled in his trap down to the harbour town
to sell his meat. He was a butcher.
Six-foot-three and very neat: high collar,
winged, a grey cravat, a waistcoat, watch-
chain just above the belt, thin narrow-
bottomed trousers, and the shoes his wife
would polish every night. He drove the trap
himself: slap of the leather reins
along the horse's back and he'd be off
with a top-hearted homburg on his head:
black English country gentleman.

Now he is dead. The meat shop burned,
his property divided. A doctor bought
the horse. His mad alsatians killed it.
The wooden trap was chipped and chopped
by friends and neighbours and used to stop-
gap fences and for firewood. One yellow
wheel was rolled across the former cowpen gate.
Only his hat is left. I 'borrowed' it.
I used to try it on and hear the night wind
man go battering through the canes, cocks waking up and thinking
it was dawn throughout the clinking country night.
Great caterpillar tractors clatter down
the broken highway now; a diesel engine grunts
where pigs once hunted garbage.
A thin asthmatic cow shares the untrashed garage.

OGUN[1]

My uncle made chairs, tables, balanced doors on, dug out
coffins, smoothing the white wood out

with plane and quick sandpaper until
it shone like his short-sighted glasses.

The knuckles of his hands were sil-
vered knobs of nails hit, hurt and flat-

tened out with blast of heavy hammer. He was knock-knee'd, flat-
footed and his clip clop sandals slapped across the concrete

flooring of his little shop where canefield mulemen and a fleet
of Bedford lorry drivers dropped in to scratch themselves and talk.

There was no shock of wood, no beam
of light mahogany his saw teeth couldn't handle.

When shaping squares for locks, a key hole
care tapped rat tat tat upon the handle

of his humpbacked chisel. Cold
world of wood caught fire as he whittled: rectangle

window frames, the intersecting x of fold-
ing chairs, triangle

trellises, the donkey
box-cart in its squeaking square.

But he was poor and most days he was hungry.
Imported cabinets with mirrors, formica table

tops, spine-curving chairs made up of tubes, with hollow
steel-like bird bones that sat on rubber ploughs,

thin beds, stretched not on boards, but blue high-tensioned cables,
were what the world preferred.

And yet he had a block of wood that would have baffled them.
With knife and gimlet care he worked away at this on Sundays,

explored its knotted hurts, cutting his way
along its yellow whorls until his hands could feel

how it had swelled and shivered, breathing air,
its weathered green burning to rings of time,

its contoured grain still tuned to roots and water.
And as he cut, he heard the creak of forests:

green lizard faces gulped, grey memories with moth
eyes watched him from their shadows, soft

liquid tendrils leaked among the flowers
and a black rigid thunder he had never heard within his hammer

came stomping up the trunks. And as he worked within his shattered
Sunday shop, the wood took shape: dry shuttered

eyes, slack anciently everted lips, flat
ruined face, eaten by pox, ravaged by rat

and woodworm, dry cistern mouth, cracked
gullet crying for the desert, the heavy black

enduring jaw; lost pain, lost iron;
emerging woodwork image of his anger.

GLOSSARY
1 *Ogun*: Yoruba and Afro-Caribbean Creator God, seen here in his aspect of divine
 craftsman.

LEOPARD

1

Caught therefore in this care-
ful cage of glint, rock,

water ringing the islands'
doubt, his

terror dares
not blink. A nervous tick-

like itch picks
at the corners of his

lips. The lean flanks quick
and quiver until the

tension cracks his
ribs. If he could only

strike or trigger
off his fury. But cunning

cold bars break his
rage, and stretched to strike

his stretched claws strike
no glory.

2

There was a land not long
ago where it was other-
wise; where he was happy.

That fatal plunge down from the
tree on antelope or duiker,[1]
was freedom for him then.

But somewhere in the dampened
dark the marks-
man watched, the strings were

stretched, the tricky traps were
ready. Yet had he felt
his supple force would fall

to such confinement,
would he, to dodge his doom
and guarantee his movement,

have paused from stalking deer
or striking down the duiker;
or would he, face to fate,

have merely murdered more?

3

But he must do
what fate had forced him to;

at birth his blood
was bent upon a flood

that forged him forward
on its deadly springs;

his paws grew heavy
and his claws shone sharp;

unleashed, his passion
slashed and mangled with its stainless

steel; no flesh he raped
would ever heal. Like grape

crushed in the mouth to you,
was each new death to him;

each death he dealt perfected him.
His victims felt this single

soft intention in him, as gentle
as a pigeon winging home.

4

Now he stands caged.
The monkeys lisp and leer
and rip and hammer
at their barriers;

he burns and paces;
turns again and paces,
disdaining admiration in those faces
that peer and pander at him

through the barriers.
Give him a tree to leap from,
liberator; in pity let him
once more move with his soft

spotted and untroubled splendour
among the thrills and whispers
of his glinting kingdom;
or unlock him and now let him

from his triggered branch
and guillotining vantage,
in one fine final falling
fall upon the quick fear-

footed deer or peer-
less antelope whose beauty,
ravaged with his sharp brutality,
propitiates the ancient guilt

each feels toward the other:
the victim's wish to hurt,
the hunter's not to;
and by this sacrifice

of strong to helpless other,
healed and aneled;[2]
both hurt and hunter
by this fatal lunge made whole.

GLOSSARY
1 *duiker*: small African antelope (from Dutch – diver, from plunging through bushes when pursued).
2 *aneled*: anointed, given extreme unction, and thus blessed and existing in a state of grace.

LABOURER

Look at his hands
cactus cracked, pricked,
worn smooth by the hoe
limestone soil's colour;
he has lost three fingers
of his left hand falling
asleep at the mill;
the black crushing grin
of the iron tooth'd ratchets
grinding the farley hill cane
have eaten him lame
and no one is to blame

the crunched bone was juicy
to the iron, there was no difference
between his knuckle joints
and ratoon shoots:[1] the soil
receives the liquor with cool flutes;
three fingers are not even worth
a stick of cane; the blood
mix does not show, the star-
gaze crystal sugar shines
no brighter for the cripple blow

and nothing more to show
for thirty years' spine-
curving labour in clear
rain, glass-eyed, coming off the sea,
fattening up the mud
in the valleys, cours-
ing down hillsides, causing the toil of the deep
well-laid roots, gripping soil,
to come steadily loose, junction and joint
between shoot and its flower to be made nonsense of

and the shame, the shame, the shame-
lessness of it all, the name-
less days in the burnt cane-
fields without love; crack of its
loud trash, spinn-
ing ashes; wrack of salt odour that will

not free his throat; the cutlass fall-
ing, fall-
ing: sweat, grit
between fingers, chigga[2]
hatching its sweet nest of pain in his toe,
and now this and now this

an old man, prickled
to sleep by the weather, his labour,
losing his hands . . .

GLOSSARY
1 *ratoon shoots*: new shoots of sugar-cane.
2 *chigga*: harvest-bug.

JOURNEYS

1

He was born where the path runs up the hill with little
children who laugh and point to the sea
and older they discover that the brittle
sand it washes is possessed by millionaires

he knew he remembered old women
who sewed old clothes by the lamp
but he couldn't remember the woman
who went to sleep in the damp

only her chair
in the corner, by the wattle under the hill
which spilled its birds in sun-
light all over the window-sill

the sun is a scourge of white, my boy,
the black night longs for the noon
there's soil for you at the end of the well
but a cow jumps over the moon

2

he went to the wrong schools;
was friendly with black faces
like his own, but was told their tales

were wrong; saw those who taught
him songs of what he ought to, what he ought
not do, take off their hats to the white

inspector's car. learn your books good,
lookin
good like him. ponds beauty cream

will lighten the skin and the black night longs for the moon
an old cracked face looks up from the well
and the dish run away with the spoon

3

so he grew up and his old instincts died like flies;
was told he should not leap the saddle
but scratch dry books to find where his spring lay

and although he did not know it then,
the historians were fools
who taught him rousseau's dictum[1] as a book affair

for behind the spectacles and speeches
behind the front rows at the speech-day plays
he watched the seas of noon-dragged aunts and mothers:
black galley slaves of prayer.

but all his thoughts were chained
which should have sparked and hammered in his brain
but that the teachers taught him not to think
of things not on curriculum

what's more
he learned that nearly all his friends
had come to be content with sub-committees
or with some bankrupt chapel in a parish of cracked bells;

that they believed a tie on sundays and a well-
brushed blazer, paved them a way to old-age heavens
paper-lined with pensions.
and older women went to funerals of girls

who died hot stretched and soft with fever
because they could not pay the doctor's fees
or were too proud to take the neighbour's gift of eggs.
and to the bleeding child's relations came the black bible'd comforters:

the lord is love, he will provide
salvation army blankets
though they could hardly dare to think
that cynthia who spat her lungs up pink

at night, would find a place beside
the parson's pampered blue eye'd child.
there'd be imperial preference up above;
eternal colour prejudice and love

4

where are the friends who ran with sunlight in their eyes
bright and upright as grass

where are they now after the young imagination
had attracted lies?

we seek we seek
but find no one to speak

the words to save
us: search

there is no destination
our prayers reach

no sun

no common sum
no good beyond our gods

of righteousness and mammon

GLOSSARY
1 *rousseau's dictum*: Jean-Jacques Rousseau (1712–78), a French philosopher and author. His best-known saying, or dictum, is: 'Man is born free but is everywhere in chains.'

SUGGESTIONS FOR WRITING AND DISCUSSION

1 *Give an account of* 'The Emigrants', *bringing out fully the connection in thought between the various sections.*
2 *Discuss parts 2 and 3 of* 'The Emigrants' *and say what you think are the differences and connections in theme and content between them.*

3 *Choose two poems or sections of poems by Brathwaite and analyse his versification (how he uses words, sounds, images, line organization, etc.) and its effect.*

4 *Using the poems selected here, illustrate two or more of the following themes Brathwaite is interested in: racism; political activism; mis-education; exploitation; identity; exile.*

5 *Give an acount of one poem or section of a poem that you find particularly effective.*

6 *'Brathwaite's poetry is most effective when it is spoken aloud.' Give your views on this point of view and use extracts from the poems here to support your argument.*

7 *'Ancestors', 'Ogun', 'Labourer'. Write about two of these poems and discuss Brathwaite's skill in describing people and work.*

8 *'Ancestors'. Compare the picture of past and present in the poem. What point is Brathwaite trying to make about the connections between past and present?*

9 *Write a poem describing someone you know or have watched carefully making or working on something (it could be a mechanic, a seamstress, a carpenter, welder, painter, a child painting model soldiers, and so on).*

FURTHER READING

The Arrivants (Rights of Passage, Masks, Islands) Edward Kamau Brathwaite (Oxford University Press)

Other Exiles Edward Kamau Brathwaite (Oxford University Press)

Mother Poem Edward Kamau Brathwaite (Oxford University Press)

DEREK WALCOTT

Derek Walcott was born in Castries, St Lucia, in 1930. Most of the island's inhabitants were French-speaking and Catholic, but Walcott's family were Protestant and English-speaking. Walcott is racially mixed, with grandfathers from the West African Gold Coast and from Warwickshire. After attending the University of the West Indies he taught for a while in Jamaica and St Lucia and then settled in Trinidad. He worked as a journalist for the Trinidad *Guardian* and in 1959 founded the Trinidad Theatre Workshop, remaining with the company until 1976.

The search for an appropriate form of English is a mark of Walcott's work; he has written in dialect and in Standard English, and in some poems has used both. He wrote in 1965:

'The West Indian poet suspects the raw spontaneity of dialect as being richer in expression, but is not willing to sacrifice the syntactical power of English. Naturally enough, where the conflict is realized, the poetry is strongest.... That dramatic ambivalence is part of what it means to be a West Indian now' (quoted by Mervyn Morris writing on Derek Walcott, in Bruce King, ed., *West Indian Literature*, Macmillan, 1979, p. 145).

Since Walcott was born and brought up on a small island, the sea plays an important part in his work. Other themes that interest him are West Indian history and politics, and time and transience. Another of the recurring concerns in his work is the relationship between black and white, between the colonizers and the colonized. Walcott has written a number of plays as well as poetry. Eliot, Pound, Dylan Thomas and Auden have all influenced him as a poet; one of the influences on him as a playwright has been the work of the Irish dramatist J. M. Synge. Walcott's work has won him many international distinctions and praise from older poets, such as Robert Graves. In 1980 he was awarded the Welsh Arts Council Poetry Prize and he toured Wales reading and talking about his poetry.

A CITY'S DEATH BY FIRE[1]

After that hot gospeller had levelled all but the churched sky,
I wrote the tale by tallow of a city's death by fire;
Under a candle's eye, that smoked in tears, I
Wanted to tell, in more than wax, of faiths that were snapped like wire.
All day I walked abroad among the rubbled tales,
Shocked at each wall that stood on the street like a liar;
Loud was the bird-rocked sky, and all the clouds were bales
Torn open by looting, and white, in spite of the fire.
By the smoking sea, where Christ walked, I asked why
Should a man wax tears, when his wooden world fails?
In town, leaves were paper, but the hills were a flock of faiths;
To a boy who walked all day, each leaf was a green breath
Rebuilding a love I thought was dead as nails,
Blessing the death and the baptism by fire.

FOOTNOTE
1 The town of Castries in St Lucia was destroyed by fire in 1948 when the poet was eighteen. Many of the houses were built of wood.

RUINS OF A GREAT HOUSE[1]

though our longest sun sets at right
declensions and makes but winter
arches, it cannot be long before we
lie down in darkness, and have our
light in ashes . . .
BROWNE: *Urn Burial*[2]

Stones only, the *disjecta membra*[3] of this Great House,
Whose moth-like girls are mixed with candledust,
Remain to file the lizard's dragonish claws;
The mouths of those gate cherubs streaked with stain.
Axle and coachwheel silted under the muck
Of cattle droppings.

                    Three crows flap for the trees,
And settle, creaking the eucalyptus boughs.
A smell of dead limes quickens in the nose
The leprosy of Empire

                    'Farewell, green fields'
                    'Farewell, ye happy groves!'

Marble as Greece, like Faulkner's south[4] in stone,
Deciduous beauty prospered and is gone;
But where the lawn breaks in a rash of trees
A spade below dead leaves will ring the bone
Of some dead animal or human thing
Fallen from evil days, from evil times.

It seems that the original crops were limes
Grown in the silt that clogs the river's skirt;
The imperious rakes are gone, their bright girls gone,
The river flows, obliterating hurt.

I climbed a wall with the grille ironwork
Of exiled craftsmen, protecting that great house
From guilt, perhaps, but not from the worm's rent,
Nor from the padded cavalry of the mouse.
And when a wind shook in the limes I heard
What Kipling[5] heard; the death of a great empire, the abuse
Of ignorance by Bible and by sword.

A green lawn, broken by low walls of stone
Dipped to the rivulet, and pacing, I thought next
Of men like Hawkins, Walter Raleigh, Drake,[6]
Ancestral murderers and poets, more perplexed
In memory now by every ulcerous crime.
The world's green age then was a rotting lime
Whose stench became the charnel galleon's text.
The rot remains with us, the men are gone.
But, as dead ash is lifted in a wind,
That fans the blackening ember of the mind,
My eyes burned from the ashen prose of Donne.[7]

Ablaze with rage, I thought
Some slave is rotting in this manorial lake,
And still the coal of my compassion fought:
That Albion[8] too, was once
A colony like ours, 'Part of the continent, piece of the main'
Nook-shotten, rook o'erblown, deranged
By foaming channels, and the vain expense
Of bitter faction.

        All in compassion ends
So differently from what the heart arranged:
'as well as if a manor of thy friend's . . .'

GLOSSARY
1 *Great House*: the mansion in which a plantation-owner lived.
2 Sir Thomas Browne (1605–82) was a philosophical writer and a practising doctor of medicine. *Urn Burial* is a meditation on funerals and death.
3 *disjecta membra*: scattered components.
4 *Faulkner's*: William Faulkner (1897–1962), American novelist who wrote about the disintegration of the American South.
5 *Kipling*: Rudyard Kipling (1865–1936), English writer who wrote about India, at that time part of the British Empire.
6 *Hawkins, Walter Raleigh, Drake*: English sea-farers who sailed the Caribbean Sea (known then as the Spanish Main) during the reign of Elizabeth I. Raleigh was also an eloquent and able poet. Sir John Hawkins (1523–95) was a naval commander who led expeditions in 1562, 1564 and 1567 to the West African and Spanish American coasts, slave-trading and fighting the Spaniards.
7 *Donne*: John Donne (1571–1631), English poet and churchman. One of his sermons contains the following lines: 'No man is an island, entire of itself; every man is a piece of the continent, a part of the main. If a clod be washed away, Europe is the less, as well as if . . . a manor of thy friend's or thine own were.'
8 *Albion*: an ancient poetical name for Britain, perhaps originating from its white cliffs (Latin 'albus') visible from the coast of Gaul.

A LESSON FOR THIS SUNDAY

The growing idleness of summer grass
With its frail kites of furious butterflies
Requests the lemonade of simple praise
In scansion gentler than my hammock swings
And rituals no more upsetting than a
Black maid shaking linen as she sings
The plain notes of some protestant hosanna
Since I lie idling from the thought in things,

Or so they should. Until I hear the cries
Of two small children hunting yellow wings,
Who break my sabbath with the thought of sin.
Brother and sister, with a common pin,
Frowning like serious lepidopterists.[1]
The little surgeon pierces the thin eyes.
Crouched on plump haunches, as a mantis prays
She shrieks to eviscerate[2] its abdomen.
The lesson is the same. The maid removes
Both prodigies from their interest in science.
The girl, in lemon frock, begins to scream
As the maimed, teetering thing attempts its flight.
She is herself a thing of summery light,
Frail as a flower in this blue August air,
Not marked for some late grief that cannot speak.

The mind swings inward on itself in fear
Swayed towards nausea from each normal sign.
Heredity of cruelty everywhere,
And everywhere the frocks of summer torn,
The long look back to see where choice is born,
As summer grass sways to the scythe's design.

GLOSSARY
1 *lepidopterists*: collectors of butterflies and moths.
2 *eviscerate*: disembowel.

A LETTER FROM BROOKLYN[1]

An old lady writes me in a spidery style,
Each character trembling, and I see a veined hand
Pellucid as paper, travelling on a skein
Of such frail thoughts its thread is often broken;
Or else the filament from which a phrase is hung
Dims to my sense, but caught, it shines like steel,
As touch a line, and the whole web will feel.
She describes my father, yet I forget her face
More easily than my father's yearly dying;
Of her I remember small, buttoned boots and the place
She kept in our wooden church on those Sundays
Whenever her strength allowed;
Grey haired, thin voiced, perpetually bowed.

'I am Mable Rawlins,' she writes, 'and know both your parents';
He is dead, Miss Rawlins, but God bless your tense:
'Your father was a dutiful, honest,
Faithful and useful person.'
For such plain praise what fame is recompense?
'A horn-painter, he painted delicately on horn,
He used to sit around the table and paint pictures.'
The peace of God needs nothing to adorn
It, nor glory nor ambition.
'He is twenty-eight years buried,'[2] she writes, 'he was called home,
And is, I am sure, doing greater work.'

The strength of one frail hand in a dim room
Somewhere in Brooklyn, patient and assured,
Restores my sacred duty to the Word.
'Home, home,' she can write, with such short time to live,
Alone as she spins the blessings of her years;
Not withered of beauty if she can bring such tears,
Nor withdrawn from the world that breaks its lovers so;
Heaven is to her the place where painters go,
All who bring beauty on frail shell or horn,
There was all made, thence their lux-mundi[3] drawn,
Drawn, drawn, till the thread is resilient steel,
Lost though it seems in darkening periods,
And there they return to do work that is God's.

So this old lady writes, and again I believe,
I believe it all, and for no man's death I grieve.

GLOSSARY
1 *Brooklyn*: a suburb of New York.
2 *twenty-eight years buried*: Walcott's father died when he and his twin brother were only one year old.
3 *lux-mundi*: the light of the world, meaning here their creative spirit.

THE TRAIN

On one hand, harrowed England,
iron, an airfield's mire,
on the other, fire-
gutted trees, a hand
raking the carriage windows.

Where was my randy white grandsire from?
He left here a century ago
to found his 'farm',
and, like a thousand others,
drunkenly seed their archipelago.
Through dirty glass
his landscape fills through my face.

Black with despair
he set his flesh on fire,
blackening, a tree of flame.
That's hell enough for here.
His blood burns through me as this engine races,
my skin sears like a hairshirt with his name.

On the bleak Sunday platform
the guiltless, staring faces
divide like tracks before me as I come.
Like you, grandfather, I cannot change places,
I am half-home.

MISSING THE SEA

Something removed roars in the ears of this house,
Hangs its drapes windless, stuns mirrors
Till reflections lack substance.

Some sound like the gnashing of windmills ground
To a dead halt;
A deafening absence, a blow.

It hoops this valley, weighs this mountain,
Estranges gesture, pushes this pencil
Through a thick nothing now,

Freights cupboards with silence, folds sour laundry
Like the clothes of the dead left exactly
As the dead behaved by the beloved,

Incredulous, expecting occupancy.

MASS MAN[1]

Through a great lion's head clouded by mange
a black clerk growls.
Next, a gold-wired peacock withholds a man,
a fan, flaunting its oval, jewelled eyes.
What metaphors!
What coruscating, mincing fantasies!

Hector Mannix, water-works clerk San Juan, has entered a lion,
Boysie, two golden mangoes bobbing for breastplates, barges[2]
like Cleopatra down her river, making style.
'Join us' they shout, 'O God, child, you can't dance?'
but somewhere in that whirlwind's radiance
a child, rigged like a bat, collapses, sobbing.

But I am dancing, look, from an old gibbet
my bull-whipped body swings, a metronome!
Like a fruit-bat[3] dropped in the silk cotton's shade
my mania, my mania is a terrible calm.

Upon your penitential morning,
some skull must rub its memory with ashes,[4]
some mind must squat down howling in your dust,
some hand must crawl and recollect your rubbish,
someone must write your poems.

GLOSSARY
1 *Mass Man*: a Carnival masquerader is called a 'mas man'. Walcott is punning on 'mas' and 'mass'. Carnival, the time of festivity before the sombre days of Lent, takes place on a number of Caribbean islands, particularly those that were once French or Spanish colonies. It is perhaps most important in Trinidad. It is a time of glittering costumes, music – especially steel bands and calypso singers – and wild revelry. Dancers and masqueraders frequently demonstrate the mixture of African and European influence in West Indian culture.
2 *barges*: a pun. Cleopatra sailed down the Nile in a barge.
3 *fruit-bat*: a fruit-eating bat.
4 *penitential morning ... ashes*: the two days of Carnival are followed by Ash Wednesday, the first day of Lent.

THE RIVER

was one, once;
reduced by circumstance
the Council tends it. Once

it could roar through town,
foul-mouthed, brown-muscled, brazenly
drunk, a raucous country-bookie,

but lately it has grown
too footloose for this settlement
of shacks, rechristened a city;

its strength wasted on gutters,
it never understood the age,
what progress meant,

so its clear, brown integument[1]
shrivelled, its tongue stutters
through the official language,

it surrenders its gutturals
to the stern, stone Victorian bridge;
reclaimed, it dies a little

daily, it crawls towards a sea
curdled with oil-slick, its force
thins like the peasantry,

it idles like those resinous
wrinkled woodsmen, the country
reek still on them, hoarse

with municipal argument,
who, falling suddenly silent
on wire-bright afternoons, reflect

on mornings when a torrent
roared down their gorges, and
no one gave a damn what the words meant.

GLOSSARY
1 *integument*: skin, covering.

ODDJOB, A BULL TERRIER[1]

You prepare for one sorrow,
but another comes.
It is not like the weather,
you cannot brace yourself,
the unreadiness is all.
Your companion, the woman,
the friend next to you,
the child at your side,
and the dog,
we tremble for them,
we look seaward and muse
it will rain.
We shall get ready for rain;
you do not connect
the sunlight altering
the darkening oleanders
in the sea-garden,
the gold going out of the palms.
You do not connect this,
the fleck of the drizzle
on your flesh
with the dog's whimper,
the thunder doesn't frighten,
the readiness is all;
what follows at your feet
is trying to tell you
the silence is all:
it is deeper than the readiness,
it is sea-deep,
earth-deep,
love-deep.

The silence
is stronger than thunder,
we are stricken dumb and deep
as the animals who never utter love
as we do, except
it becomes unutterable
and must be said,
in a whimper,
in tears,
in the drizzle that comes to our eyes
not uttering the loved thing's name,
the silence of the dead,
the silence of the deepest buried love is
the one silence,
and whether we bear it for beast,
for child, for woman, or friend,
it is the one love, it is the same,
and it is blest
deepest by loss
it is blest, it is blest.

FOOTNOTE
1 Oddjob is the name of a dog that belonged to friends of Walcott.

SUGGESTIONS FOR WRITING AND DISCUSSION

1 *Write a critical account of* 'Ruins of a Great House', *paying particular attention to the imagery relating to time, and Walcott's treatment of the past and its relation to the present.*
2 *Write an account of* 'A Letter from Brooklyn'. *Show why the letter and the writer have such a deep effect on the poet. Outline the central ideas in the poem and discuss Walcott's techniques: his use of direct speech, rhyme, imagery.*
3 *Compare Walcott's treatment of the past in two of his poems.*
4 *'The River'. Describe the changes that have taken place to the river and its surroundings. In what ways is this both a critical and a humorous poem?*
5 *Choose the poem by Walcott that appeals to you the most and give reasons for your choice.*
6 *Write your own poem about an old building or a river, stream, canal, or wood in your area and show how time has changed it – for better or for worse.*

FURTHER READING

Selected Poems Derek Walcott (Heinemann Educational Books)
Collected Poems Dylan Thomas (Dent)

ZULFIKAR GHOSE

Zulfikar Ghose was born in
Sialkot, in what is now Pakistan,
in 1935. He went to England in
1952 and studied at Keele
University. He worked as a
cricket correspondent and a
teacher before his first volume
of poems was published in 1964.
He has written an
autobiography entitled
Confessions of a Native-Alien.
More recently he has lived in the
USA and South America. He
has written a number of novels
with South American settings.
Since 1969 he has been
Associate Professor of English
Literature at the University of
Texas, Austin.

Many of Ghose's poems describe
memories of childhood and
family life in Pakistan. Others
deal with the feelings of an
immigrant in England, someone
who is divided between two

worlds. They express a sense of
alienation and the uprootedness
of someone who is a product of
at least two cultures. His view of
the world is sharp and clinical,
without sentimentality, and his
poems often express a wry, dry
humour.

UNCLE AYUB

'You belong here,' grandma cried. 'Here, here, here!'
beating her breast. Uncle Ayub, her youngest son,
watched aeroplanes, longed to join the War.
But grandma sat in the courtyard, the sun
driving tears from her body: would not eat
or speak. Her body was her final threat.

Uncle Ayub and I had secret plans.
Brushing fluff from my sailor suit I tapped
my chest for his promised medals, stuck pins
to keep an imitation army cap
on my head. Bring me real bullets, I said,
Uncle, bring me soldiers, alive or dead.

For grandma the war was at home: to keep
her one unmarried son where she could kiss
him good night. She had a locked-up chest deep
with yards of satin, perfumes – gifts kept in case
of need. I feared she would lock my uncle
up till he dried like a dung-cake on the wall.

The War ended. Grandma smiled, and made me wash
with soap someone had brought her from Paris
twenty years ago. Uncle Ayub thought of cash
and a wife. Now there would be no more wars.
He left home soon after the marriage feast,
and began a business in the Middle East.

THE CROWS

Crows will stick their beaks into anything.
Ugliness protects them: children don't care
to pet them, and when they descend on trees,
eagles discreetly go somewhere quieter.

They will sit on balconies and appear
to comment on passing traffic. Their black
cloak never conceals the dagger of speech,
their communal weapon. They talk, talk, talk.

I've heard them break the silence of night
with sudden loud cawing as if provoked
into dispute by a falling star,
and then flying skywards as though to look

up some evidence, keen as scientists;
yet really, when you see their missions
come mostly to nothing, they appear more
like intensely dedicated politicians.

THIS LANDSCAPE, THESE PEOPLE

1

My eighth spring in England I walk among
   the silver birches of Putney Heath,
   stepping over twigs and stones: being stranger,
   I see but do not touch: only the earth
   permits an attachment. I do not wish
to be seen, and move, eyes at my sides, like a fish.

And do they notice me, I wonder, these
   Englishmen strolling with stiff country strides?
   I lean against a tree, my eyes are knots
   in its bark, my skin the wrinkles in it sides.
   I leap hedges, duck under chestnut boughs,
and through the black clay let my swift heels trail like ploughs.

A child at a museum, England for me
   is an exhibit within a glass case.
   The country, like an antique chair, has a rope
   across it. I may not sit, only pace
   its frontiers. I slip through ponds, jump ditches,
through galleries of ferns see England in pictures.

2

My seventeen years in India I swam
   along the silver beaches of Bombay,
   pulled coconuts from the sky, and tramped
   red horizons with the swagger and sway
   of Romantic youth; with the impudence
of a native tongue, I cried for independence.

A troupe came to town, marched through villages;
   began with two tight-rope walkers, eyes gay
   and bamboos and rope on their bare shoulders;
   a snake charmer joined them, beard long and grey,
   baskets of cobras on his turbaned head;
through villages marched: children, beating on drums, led

them from village to village, and jugglers
   joined them and swallowers of swords, eaters
   of fire brandishing flames through the thick air,
   jesters with tongues obscene as crows', creatures
   of the earth: stray dogs, lean jackals, a cow;
stamping, shouting, entertaining, make a row

from village to village they marched to town:
   conjurers to bake bread out of earth, poets
   to recite epics at night. The troupe, grown
   into a nation, halted, squirmed: the sets
   for its act, though improvised, were re-cast
from the frames of an antique, slow-moving, dead past.

India halted: as suddenly as a dog,
   barking, hangs out his tongue, stifles his cry.
   An epic turned into a monologue
   of death. The rope lay stiff across the country;
   all fires were eaten, swallowed all the swords;
the horizons paled, then thickened, blackened with crows.

Born to this continent, all was mine
    to pluck and taste: pomegranates to purple
    my tongue and chillies to burn my mouth. Stones
    were there to kick. This landscape, these people –
    bound by the rope, consumed by their fire.
Born here, among these people, I was a stranger.

3

This landscape, these people! Silver birches
    with polished trunks chalked around a chestnut.
    All is fall-of-night still. No thrush reaches
    into the earth for worms, nor pulls at the root
    of a crocus. Dogs have led their masters home.
I stroll, head bowed, hearing only the sound of loam

at my heel's touch. Now I am intimate
    with England; we meet, secret as lovers.
    I pluck leaves and speak into the air's mouth;
    as a woman's hair, I deck with flowers
    the willow's branches; I sit by the pond,
my eyes are stars in its stillness; as with a wand,

I stir the water with a finger until
    it tosses waves, until countries appear
    from its dark bed: the road from Putney Hill
    runs across oceans into the harbour
    of Bombay. To this country I have come.
Stranger or an inhabitant, this is my home.

AN ATTACHMENT TO THE SUN

We sat eating fruit, a tangerine first,
peeling London's frost for a tropical grove:
our convivial attachment to the sun
is also our love.

Suddenly she laughed. A rush of glow-worms
breathed in her eyes. The window, lined with ice,
unbuttoned a row of geraniums
gay as butterflies.

I broke two walnuts in my palm. Lizards
clicked their tongues in her mouth. We tricked
the weather with love, made London a suburb
of the Tropics.

AN IMPERIAL EDUCATION

The P. & O. liner docked in Tilbury[1]
and I who'd been looking for Wordsworth's landscapes
(since the old Empire still educated the new India)
    saw instead the blurred shapes
        of a wet April day: a drear
England appeared of cranes, warehouses and silvery

    railway tracks. At London
Bridge, I leaned over the murky, embittered
Thames, taking an old-fashioned Eng. Lit. view,
    not seeing the littered
        river but some dew-
drenched willow branches hanging over a sylvan

    stream a Blackie[2] textbook
had made me long for in a Bombay classroom.
I walked the streets of London with a pensive
    face, a posture assumed
        from some page in *Palgrave*[3]
or a Millais[4] reproduction, calculated to look

    similar to the shepherds
returning from the meadows of their offices
to their bedsitting cottages in South Ken.[5]
    All my suits were three-piece
        pinstripe with a red carnation
in the buttonhole. Swallows were all the birds

    I saw, daffodils all
the flowers. I wouldn't drink beer because I'd
been told that young men only drank sherry.
    A Byron from Bombay, I sighed,
        looked sad and world-weary.
Peter Sellers' Indian was less comical

than my rendering
of English customs. The naïve, confused
and clueless East died slowly. Imitative
and sycophantic, used
to a century of submissive
bowing, the Indian, always when 'God Save the King'

was played, stood more erect
than the Englishman. That and Macaulay[6]
were my education. Now I wonder what immigrants
arriving in Southall[7] say
about their long acquaintance
with the English way of life which they must suspect

of a subtle corruption,
being run by Fagins and Artful Dodgers.[8] Well,
dear English reader, know that whether it's Delhi's
sudden dismissal
of the BBC,[9] or Shelley's
words in my mouth, it's all due to Imperial Education.

GLOSSARY
1 *Tilbury*: London docks.
2 *Blackie*: an educational publisher.
3 *Palgrave*: a reference to *Palgrave's Golden Treasury*, a famous anthology of English verse.
4 *Millais*: a French painter of peasant and country life.
5 *South Ken*: South Kensington, an area of London.
6 *Macaulay*: a nineteenth-century English historian.
7 *Southall*: part of London near Heathrow airport where many Asians settled when they came to Britain.
8 *Fagins and Artful Dodgers*: criminal characters in Charles Dickens's *Oliver Twist*.
9 *Delhi's . . . the BBC*: when India became independent it set up its own broadcasting system.

IN THE DESERT

When grandma took me to Quetta[1]
the train cut through sugarcane
and maize fields across the Punjab
and entered the Thar desert.

I stood at the window for hours
and watched the sand of the desert
meet the sandy beach of the sky
where the heat-haze broke in waves.

It was the first time that I'd seen
a world in which there seemed
nothing to live for and nothing
with which to keep one alive.

I had a fantasy as children do
of being alone in the desert
and lasting there for no longer
than a drop of water.

I stood at the window for hours
and wanted to know for how long
the world as far as I could see
would continue completely empty.

Now thirty years later when I look back
on that journey through the desert
I feel I am still at the window
searching the horizon for plants.

GLOSSARY
1 *Quetta*: a town in the north of Pakistan.

THE PRESERVATION OF LANDSCAPES

Again summer journeys across England
take me past landscapes become familiar
with five years' travelling. The country comes
alive again with its beeches and elms,
composing its prettiness in my mind
with a fleeting abstraction of colour.

Gliders, pinned to the sky above Cambridge,
are still as eagles for a moment, then
are swift as the homeward flight of swallows.
I drive across the flat Cambridgeshire farms
and find the sun absorbed in a lonely
colloquy with the land, bargaining growth.

The train does ninety on the run between
Leicester and Derby, leaps across the Trent,
and, as a plane overshoots a runway,
briefly avoids industrial Midlands
to nibble through pastureland, devouring
the coarse grass with the quickness of locusts.

Dark pine-forests on the road to Portsmouth;
aspens, whose leaves catch the breeze and the light
as do sequins on a hat at Ascot,
and the gay ash-trees on the road to Bath;
and the fields, the fields are like coloured bits
of paper pasting England on my mind.

I share the anxiety of Englishmen
about England, prizing each field, each tree,
each tuft of grass above the incursions
of concrete and steel. O, sad, sad, England!
The beeches in East Riding, too, among the moors,
are yellow with the dust from upturned roads.

And yet I would rather have steel, rather
go giddy on winding car-park buildings
than look at the fiercely sunlit landscapes
of Southeast Asia where foreign jets
have cut the jungle for airstrips and the earth
is cleaved at the centre, deflowered with bombs.

GEOGRAPHY LESSON

When the jet sprang into the sky,
it was clear why the city
had developed the way it had,
seeing it scaled six inches to the mile.
There seemed an inevitability
about what on ground had looked haphazard,
unplanned and without style
when the jet sprang into the sky.

When the jet reached ten thousand feet,
it was clear why the country
had cities where rivers ran
and why the valleys were populated.
The logic of geography –
that land and water attracted man –
was clearly delineated
when the jet reached ten thousand feet.

When the jet rose six miles high,
it was clear that the earth was round
and that it had more sea than land.
But it was difficult to understand
that the men on the earth found
causes to hate each other, to build
walls across cities and to kill.
From that height, it was not clear why.

DECOMPOSITION

I have a picture I took in Bombay
of a beggar asleep on the pavement:
grey-haired, wearing shorts and a dirty shirt,
his shadow thrown aside like a blanket.

His arms and legs could be cracks in the stone,
routes for the ants' journeys, the flies' descents.
Brain-washed by the sun into exhaustion,
he lies veined into stone, a fossil man.

Behind him, there is a crowd passingly
bemused by a pavement trickster and quite
indifferent to this very common sight
of an old man asleep on the pavement.

I thought it then a good composition
and glibly called it *The Man in the Street*,
remarking how typical it was of
India that the man in the street lived there.

His head in the posture of one weeping
into a pillow chides me now for my
presumption at attempting to compose
art out of his hunger and solitude.

SUGGESTIONS FOR WRITING AND DISCUSSION

1 *Describe some of the differences Ghose found between life in Pakistan and life in England, using illustrations and examples from his poems.*
2 *Many of Ghose's poems are about journeys. Choose two of them and compare and contrast the experiences described.*
3 *Write an account of 'An Imperial Education', making clear the poet's attitudes and intention in writing the poem.*
4 *Comment on Ghose's skill as a poet in making the subjects he writes about interesting.*
5 *Imagine you are arriving in India or Pakistan for the first time. Write a poem entitled 'Stranger' or 'First Day'.*
6 *Read Ghose's poem 'Uncle Ayub'; consider the way in which he describes his grandmother, his uncle and himself. Try your own poem about the interaction of two or three members of your family.*

FURTHER READING

The Loss of India Zulfikar Ghose (Routledge & Kegan Paul)
The Violent West Zulfikar Ghose (Macmillan)
Jets from Orange Zulfikar Ghose (Macmillan)

GENERAL SUGGESTIONS FOR WRITING AND DISCUSSION

1 *Compare three poems by three different poets which describe people.*
2 *Choose two satirical poems by two different poets and compare them, for instance, Plomer's 'A Fall of Rock' and Walcott's 'The River'.*
3 *Compare two poems about animals by different poets.*
4 *Write about three poems which deal with relations between black and white people and say what you have learned from them. You could use, for instance, poems by McKay and sections from Brathwaite's 'The Emigrants', Birney's 'For George Lamming', or Walcott's 'Ruins of a Great House'.*
5 *Compare the poems of two poets who have written about 'personal feelings', for instance, Dennis Brutus and Gabriel Okara.*
6 *Choose the poet who has impressed and interested you most and give reasons for your choice.*
7 *Choose two poets who seem to you very different in style and approach and explain the differences between them.*
8 *Discuss two poems about a place or a scene and point out the differences and similarities (if there are any) between the poets' approach and techniques. For instance, does the writer concentrate on describing the scene, or use it as a means of starting off a discussion or presenting a set of ideas? (Possible poems to use are: 'Nightsong: City', 'South', 'The Snowflakes Sail Gently Down', 'Takakkaw Falls'.)*
9 *Choose one or more social and political topics that you feel are very important. Write a poem or set of poems around these topics. (You could refer again to the political poems by McKay, Brathwaite and Brutus.) Decide whether the poems are meant to be read silently or are for reading aloud.*
10 *Prepare a poetry programme (using poems in this collection) and tape-record it as a presentation for the rest of the class. You could make a thematic collection around a topic such as 'People', 'Outcasts', 'Struggle', 'Past and Present', or you could take a single poet's work, or you could select contrasting poems, or, simply, the poems you like best. One person should be the presenter and the poems can be read and introduced by members of the group.*
11 *Select and prepare poems from the collection for a reading to be done as a poetry session with another class. Include your own poems written by members of the group after reading poems in the collection.*
12 *Choose a number of poems for display and choose photographs, newspaper cuttings, drawings, and so on, to go with the poems. Here again your display could be thematic or based on a particular poet.*